Learning Strategies for Adults

Sandra C. Crux

To Jacqueline, in her memory

To Andy, for his ongoing struggle with learning disabilities

Learning Strategies for Adults

Compensations for Learning Disabilities

Sandra C. Crux

WE

Wall & Emerson, Inc.

Toronto, Ontario • Middletown, Ohio

Requests for permission to make copies of any part of this work should be sent
to:
Wall & Emerson, Inc., Six O'Connor Drive, Toronto, Ontario, Canada M4K 2K1

Orders for this book may be directed to either of the following addresses:

For the United States:	*For Canada and the rest of the world:*
Wall & Emerson, Inc.	Wall & Emerson, Inc.
806 Central Ave.	Six O'Connor Drive
P. O. Box 448686	Toronto, Ontario, Canada
Middletown, Ohio 45044-8686	M4K 2K1

By telephone or facsimile (for both addresses):

Telephone: (416) 467-8685
Fax: (416) 696-2460

Canadian Cataloguing in Publication Data

Crux, Sandra C.
    Learning strategies for adults

Includes bibliographical references and index.
ISBN 1-895131-04-9

1. Adult learning. 2. Learning disabilities.
3. Study, Method of. I. Title.

LC5219.C78 1991   371.92'6   C91-093369-3

ISBN 1-895131-04-9
Printed in Canada.
    2 3 4 5   94 93

Table of Contents

4. Goal Setting and Time Management   71

List of Figures

Preface

This book was written for practitioners. I have tried to make the presentation of the various compensatory learning strategies, found in Chapters 3 through 6, practical and straightforward. I have also introduced an informal diagnostic process which I call HELP (an acronym for *Holistic Educational Literacy Process*), an easy-to-follow assessment method for adult educators in a variety of settings where formal assessment is not feasible or practical. The HELP method came out of a need expressed by adult educators in the field for a simple yet accurate diagnostic procedure to identify literacy-related learning problems.

Many of the ideas and suggestions outlined in the chapters on compensatory strategies are the result of some twenty years in the field of education and learning disabilities, both personally and professionally. Professionally, I became acquainted with learning disabilities and the concept of cognitive learning strategies during my years teaching elementary and secondary school in the 1970s and early 1980s, and later, during my doctoral training at the Ontario Institute for Studies in Education at the University of Toronto. My personal experiences with learning disabilities are as a result of my role as a parent and predate my professional work. I became painfully aware of the characteristics and consequences of learning disabilities after my son was born in the late 1960s. Having both a personal and professional awareness of learning difficulties has given me, I believe, a unique perspective, and one which has motivated me to find learning methods that make it possible for people with severe learning problems to move toward their educational or occupational potential.

I have also learned much from my colleagues and students, as well as my clients, in my capacity as an adult learning and assessment consultant in private practice and as an adjunct professor with the Faculty of Education at Brock University and the Centre for Language Studies at Niagara College, both in Ontario, Canada. Particularly, a special word of thanks to the following people: to Patrick O'Neill for co-authoring an article with me on the topic of learning strategies, the impetus that got me started in this direction; to Jim Wagner, for his insights on literacy-related assessment procedures and practices; and to all those involved in the pilot-testing of an early draft of this manuscript, namely, Marian Walsh and Joy Hutton, and their community college instructors involved in a special education professional development program, and, the staff and students connected with the English Department's Centre for Language Studies "peer-tutoring" training program at Niagara College during the fall of 1990.

Appreciation to my publisher/editors, Martha and Byron Wall, for their belief in this project, their constancy and support. As well, a word of acknowledgement to: my husband Jim, who is, and always has been, supportive of my endeavors; to my daughter, Carole, son-in-law, Chuck, and son, Andy, for their love and encouragement; to my grandchildren, Julia and Matthew, for their energy and enthusiasm when I needed a break during the preparation of this book; and to my mother, for being a career role model.

I invite readers to try the HELP informal assessment method as well as the compensation strategies and environmental supports presented here, and to correspond with me in care of the publisher to let me know how they work for them.

Sandra C. Crux
January 1991

1

An Introduction to Compensatory Methods and Strategies

Purpose

This handbook is intended for adult educators who find that the instructional techniques used in the past are no longer effective. A knowledge of compensatory methods is essential for teaching the increasing numbers of adult students with literacy-related learning disabilities who are enroling in further education, job training, or vocational rehabilitation courses.

Most universities and community colleges in Canada, the United States, and abroad have counseling and special-needs departments which have personnel with specialized training and access to a variety of special arrangements and supports. Yet, there is still little concrete information available to show practitioners how to match learning problems with programming solutions.

The purposes of this handbook are threefold:

- to clarify the assessment process;
- to outline and describe a variety of compensatory strategies and supports that can help learning disabled people;
- to be useful as a textbook in adult education, counseling, or learning disabilities programs in occupational training, continuing education, or higher education.

Audience

The audience to whom this book is directed is diverse. The compensatory strategies, supports, and technical aids presented can be used by:

- teachers of adults participating in basic skills training, vocational retraining, or secondary school upgrading programs;
- community college, university, or other higher education faculty and staff; and
- instructors in many adult education training courses (e.g. rehabilitation and literacy trainers, or occupational and human resource personnel involved in staff development).

Organization

This book contains six chapters. The balance of Chapter 1 presents some essential definitions and descriptions, and sets out the direction for the whole book. Included are:

- the use of the terms "adult educator" and "adult learner";
- the criteria for a learning disability;
- the explanation of confusing language surrounding the terms: learning strategies, cognitive strategies, accommodations, aids, and technical supports;
- the purpose of informal assessment;
- the ways to teach adult learners the various strategies; and
- the principles of adult education that underlie this book.

Chapter 2 examines the assessment process and the formulation of hypotheses about learning problems and programming. A brief explanation of formal assessment procedures will be offered as it is important for special needs and rehabilitation counselors to know on what basis certain recommendations are made. In Chapter 2 HELP, an informal assessment method, will also be described. Developed and pilot-tested by myself, the purpose of HELP is to give adult educators concrete and reliable information on which to base positive and practical programming ideas and suggestions. When used by those who have some counseling, special education, or adult education training, HELP can provide an effective informal diagnostic method for matching specific learning problems with specific compensatory strategies. At the end of each of the eight steps of HELP, outlined in Chapter 2, a practical point-form list of possible characteristics of learning disabilities is provided under the heading *Results Indicating Problems,* as well as the headings *Possible Formal Instruments,* and *Where to Find Strategies.*

Chapters 3 through 6 include descriptions of various instructional and programming techniques and strategies, with explanations of how they should be used. Each of these four chapters focuses on different techniques and strategies: Chapter 3 on environmental supports, both general and instructional, Chapter 4 on goal setting and time management methods, Chapter 5 on reading fluency and comprehension strategies, and Chapter 6 on notetaking and written language approaches.

At the beginning of each of these four chapters are helpful summaries, contained in Figures 3–1, 4–1, 5–1, and 6–1. The layout of these outlines is as follows:

- The left column itemizes the learning disabilities discussed in the chapter.
- The middle column presents programming ideas to compensate for the problems itemized in the left column. These suggestions are directed to special needs or human resource personnel who are in a position to provide one-on-one educational counseling.
- The right column lists practical instructional techniques and methods to compensate for the same disabilities, and is directed to instructors and trainers teaching in both small or large group situations.

Verification

The effectiveness and applicability of the strategies and techniques discussed in this handbook have been verified by:

- examining research in adult education, educational psychology, and learning disabilities;
- pilot-testing and ongoing use in the author's private practice as an adult learning consultant involved in assessment and diagnosis, both formal and informal, and learning strategies compensatory programming;
- feedback from adult educators working and teaching in the field who are using HELP and the strategies discussed in this book; and
- a pilot-project conducted at Niagara College of Applied Arts and Sciences during the 1990/1991 academic year in a course, sponsored by the English Department's Centre for Language Studies, entitled "Peer-Tutoring Language Skills." This course trained students to be

peer tutors of other students whose learning disabilities interfered with successful completion of the compulsory English course.

Terminology

Adult Educator and Adult Learner

In this handbook, the term "adult educators" refers to those individuals who are guiding learners towards an understanding of the content or skills in a particular subject or specialty area, the acquisition of reading and writing skills, and a knowledge of when to use compensatory support strategies. The term "adult learners" in this book refers to people with learning disabilities.

Learning Disabilities

Learning disabilities are difficulties in learning which require instructional and learning compensations. According to the US National Joint Committee of Learning Disabilities, a learning disability refers to a varied but related group of disorders shown by difficulties in either listening, speaking, reading, writing, reasoning, or mathematical abilities. In addition, these disorders must be *intrinsic* to the individual and are presumed to be due to a central nervous system dysfunction and not another cause such as environmental disadvantage or a developmental handicap (Hammill, Leigh, McNutt & Larsen, 1981, 336).

A formal educational assessment is usually the only recognized way to decide whether or not a learning problem is intrinsic to the individual as a result of a central nervous system disorder. Sometimes learners' problems are so severe or puzzling that a formal assessment is necessary.

However, the process of formal identification is both time-consuming and costly, and access to such testing is often impossible for many individuals who are most in need of support services. Formal assessments and diagnoses are especially difficult to obtain in non-profit literacy and industrial training settings. Therefore, it would be helpful if the effectiveness and appropriateness of some forms of informal testing were also recognized.

There are some learning difficulties that are beyond the scope of this handbook. These include attention deficit disorders, social problems, developmental handicaps, autism, schizophrenia, stroke, and traumatic brain injury. Identification, prognosis and recommendations for these conditions should be obtained only under the supervision of registered psychologists or appropriate medical personnel.

However, the HELP assessment process and compensatory programs have been used in my practice with people who are survivors of traumatic brain injury as a result of an accident. These methods appear to work in much the same way as they do for people with learning disabilities.

Compensatory Strategies

Before learners can compensate for weaknesses, they first must be aware of what they do poorly (Kronick & Smith 1988, 5). When they know this, they must be prepared to analyze what goes wrong and where the breakdown occurs. With that information, alternative approaches can be considered. These alternative methods are called *compensatory strategies.*

However, just as the term "learning disabilities" is complex and difficult to define, so is the term "compensatory strategies."

In the literature on learning disabilities and related topics, compensatory methods or strategies often may be referred to as compensatory aids, compensatory or environmental supports and accommodations, study strategies, cognitive strategies, and learning strategies. Although there are some variations in their characteristics, the purpose of all these aids and strategies is similar—to provide ways of compensating for a learning problem.

There are also several instructional techniques and methods that can be used by instructors or trainers to help people with learning disabilities master content and/or skills, and discover *how* to learn more effectively on their own (Alley & Deshler, 1979).

Compensatory supports include "aids," "environmental accommodations," and "special arrangements." *Compensatory aids* are technical devices such as tape recorders, earphones, computer word processors, computer-based spelling programs, or visual screens. An aid is also a person, such as an instructor, notetaker, editor, or reader. The term *environmental accommodations* can also refer to these types of aids but usually alludes to a variety of special arrangements, such as taped textbooks, oral or take-home tests, final examinations completed in a quiet room, or alternative seating.

Compensation strategies include both *study strategies* and *cognitive strategies* and are often called learning strategies, or may be referred to as spatial, elaborative, organizational, or generative strategies. They provide effective methods for processing information when thinking, remembering, storing, and making sense out of old and new information, all of which are essential skills required for listening, speaking, reading, and writing effectively, as well as problem solving and making decisions. Cognitive strategies help people develop memory capacity, expand new information, and connect it with existing knowledge. For example, they make it possible for readers to understand what they have read by connecting and linking what is read with previously acquired knowledge. It is important to be able to remember and connect or *link* that old information with the new incoming information (Anderson, 1985, Mayer, 1987, Norman, 1982). For example, two cognitive strategies, called *chunking* and *association,* are often used to memorize telephone numbers or postal codes. Using *chunking*, numbers are learned by grouping digits in sets of twos or threes. Another simple example of chunking is the childhood alphabet song, where all the letters are sung in groups. Using *association*, numbers are paired with some previous knowledge, such as age or children's birthdays. (Mayer, 1987). Most of us automatically use cognitive strategies and cannot remember how we learned them. Unfortunately, learning disabled people usually don't learn or use these strategies without intervention.

Since each cognitive skill or ability is based on previous learning, students need to command a broad, flexible, and appropriate range of skills in order to learn something new. Think of the prerequisite skills involved in learning how to divide numbers—knowledge of addition, subtraction, and multiplication. In order to learn to read and write, one must know the alphabet. For more advanced reading and writing, e.g. preparing college assignments, learners need prerequisite skills in researching, analyzing, and summarizing. Whether computing mathematically, listening to a lecture, or reading and writing, people must be able to elaborate or build new knowledge by recalling what they already know and linking to it. Cognitive strategies are the tools we need to be able to think, remember, and make sense of our world.

Instructional techniques are both supports and strategies that can be used by all adult educators regardless of the setting. These compensatory techniques are listed in Figures 3–1, 4–1, 5–1, and 6–1. These techniques are particularly helpful to practitioners because they are concrete approaches and within the control of the trainer: for example, using audio-visual equipment, detailed course outlines, or advance organizers.

To Sum Up Terminology

- *Compensatory supports* are technical and external aids or accommodations, such as taped textbooks, audio-visual supports, and computer programs, or special arrangements for taking tests.
- *Compensatory strategies* describe study, cognitive, spatial, memory, or learning strategies.
- *Instructional techniques* refer to approaches and methods that can be used by teachers and trainers in one-on-one and small or large groups to help students or personnel learn the content or skills expected.

About Learning and the Learning Disabled Adult

Memory Capacity

Without memory, learning is not possible. We need only look at people with Alzheimer's disease to recognize the debilitating effects of damage to the memory on intellectual capacity. Although not nearly as severe, adult learners with learning disabilities usually have memory-related deficits in attention span and storage or retrieval of information.

An example of the complexity of memory processing is the act of driving a car. Imagine yourself behind the wheel of your car. What do you think about? Do you have to recall all the rules of the road every time you start your car? Obviously not. And, when you see a sign while you are driving, you know instantly what it means and act accordingly. Where does that knowledge come from? How did it get there in the first place?

Well, before driving a vehicle you obtained a beginner's permit by passing a preliminary test. In order to learn the rules and regulations for this test, you had to study and memorize them. This required you to pay attention to what you were reading and memorize the information for later recall.

There are three storage areas in our memory. Mayer (1988) refers to these three areas as sensory memory (SM), short-term memory (STM), and long-term memory (LTM). Information processed during your first exposure to the rules of the road was stored in your sensory memory (SM). But, since information in this area fades rapidly, you had to continue to attend. By attending to a particular piece of information, it was transferred to your short-term memory (STM).

There are two interdependent information processing systems in short-term memory (STM). One is referred to as *episodic* memory, which receives and stores information that is temporally dated. The other, *semantic* memory, makes spatial connections among temporal events, and is necessary for the use of language, making connections and organizing knowledge into rules. When you were learning the rules of the road, that information was stored around the time you memorized those rules. Think about the time you learned those facts. When the memory comes to your consciousness, are you recalling that information as you think about it today, or in the words and emotions of the young adult or adolescent you were at the time you memorized it? Whatever the case, and whether or not you can remember the time or events surrounding your learning the traffic and safety rules, that knowledge was processed in short-term memory (STM) prior to being transferred to long-term memory (LTM).

Although no example is ever perfect, acknowledging how we can retrieve information we learned a long time ago is helpful in understanding how difficulties with information processing systems can influence the memorizing capacities of people with learning disabilities. If information cannot be adequately processed, stored, or retrieved, learning becomes difficult, if not nearly impossible.

Learning Styles

The adult education and related literature contains much on the connection between personality type and learning or leadership style (cf. Kolb, 1984). In cognitive processing terms, learning style is a preference for receiving or processing information through one sensory modality over the other. In practical terms, it is a preference for taking in and processing information successively, simultaneously, or verbatim. In the context of this book, the term "learning style" refers to a cognitive preference for learning in one or more of three ways:

- through auditory presentations and abstract reasoning;
- through visual presentations and abstract reasoning; or,
- through auditory and visual presentations and simple memorization and rote, combined with a preference for either the auditory or visual modality.

Since we hear words and sentences in sequence, it is logical that people with an auditory learning style preference like to use lists and diagrams that outline facts and concepts in a sequential manner. To set up categories or hierarchically organized sequential formats successfully requires the ability to conceptualize, analyze, and synthesize.

Individuals who prefer visual processing, which also requires advanced abilities to elaborate, connect, and transfer information, prefer to take in facts and concepts simultaneously. They learn best from pictures or images, such as graphic organizers (Johnson, 1987a; Luria, 1966; and Masland, 1976).

A reliance on rote memorization or assimilating information verbatim, which requires few abstract reasoning abilities, reflects immaturity or learning deficits in auditory or visual processing abilities. Schmeck (1988) labels this learning style "shallow," because learners simply describe or literally reproduce what was studied. This is not to suggest that people preferring this learning style cannot process information; obviously, they can if they are able to memorize information word for word. However, they have not been able to learn to use their sensory modalities effectively to expand and examine what they are learning.

Understanding this concept of learning styles and their influence on how well learning disabled people perform can be illuminating for the adult educators trying to help them. For example, many instructors and trainers find that their learning disabled participants have serious problems with notetaking and written language, in trying to decide what to include or what to leave out during lectures or when writing a summary of a reading passage. Since the compensatory strategies often used in this case, sequential or visual organizers, and sentence combining, require the prerequisite skills of synthesizing and summarizing, training has to back up to the point where participants are performing. Therefore, it is helpful to know how learners prefer to learn. Educators can find this out during the administration of the informal assessment tool, HELP (e.g. during Step 5).

Motivation and Perseverance

For successful results, learner motivation and perseverance are absolutely essential when implementing an individualized compensatory strategies program (Snow, 1989). They are prerequisite attitude components for the success of any such program. If, for example, learners are referred to counselors against their will or inclination, the likelihood of success will be reduced significantly. It is very important that learners are self-motivated or helped to become that way before programs are under way. However, if necessary, it is possible to begin with a modified program in order to show learners that the strategies do work. Even small successes can motivate learners to continue.

Classroom instructors and trainers need a measure of motivation and perseverance as well when trying new compensatory instructional techniques and methods. It is not easy to change the way we develop and present what we teach, or the way we teach it. But in order to reach all students, whether they have identified or assumed learning disabilities, experiment with the strategies presented throughout this handbook. Do not try to make too many changes at one time; the amount of work involved could become overwhelming. Just as learners become motivated to try new challenges when they have experienced success, so will instructors when they discover that these instructional methods work!

The Role of Assessment

The success of matching compensatory strategies to adult learners' particular problems depends on how well adult educators diagnose what learning disabilities are involved. Sometimes this is as simple a matter as noting that learners cannot spell on their written assignments. Then, instructors and trainers might recommend the use of a word processing program with a spellcheck, or refer participants to a special needs counselor for individualized help. Or, learners may simply need to *hear* and *see* information at the same time, and the use of an overhead projector and/or an advance organizer during a class lecture or presentation will suffice. At other times, problems are either not as obvious or much more severe, and program recommendations and accommodations are not so easy.

Since the role of assessment is crucial for successful programming and many of us are not qualified to conduct formal assessment procedures, HELP, an informal diagnostic test, will be presented in Chapter 2. It can be administered by instructors and trainers, special needs personnel in higher education, or counselors in industrial or governmental settings.

Types of Compensatory Strategies

This handbook presents four different categories of instructional and compensatory strategies:

- environmental supports and study skills;
- goal setting and time management strategies;
- reading fluency and comprehension strategies; and,
- notetaking and written language strategies.

Environmental Support and Study Skills:

People with learning disabilities tend to get lost more often than the rest of us. In learning environments they often do not know where to go for help, or find it difficult to be assertive and to explain their learning needs (Blalock and Johnson, 1987; Vogel, 1987).

Methods are suggested in Chapter 3 that help participants:

- learn how to get around the physical environment;
- learn where to go for the services and help they need; and,
- learn when it is appropriate to ask for such assistance.

Also outlined in Chapter 3 are instructor-based techniques and environmental supports, such as creative and multisensory ways to use audio-visual equipment to enable teachers and trainers to reach their learning disabled students by improving the effectiveness of their classroom presentation practices. And finally, student study strategies are discussed, including the following:

- a library skills procedure;
- SCORER, a method to help students learn how to take formal examinations; and
- practical ways of managing course materials (Towle, 1982; Vogel, 1987).

Goal Setting and Time Management

Chapter 4 presents goal setting and timetabling strategies designed to help learning disabled adults:

- organize available time more effectively;
- set realistic immediate, short-term or long-term goals;
- use course outlines as the basis for time management planning.

Reading Fluency and Comprehension

Chapter 5 presents compensatory strategies that can be used in all settings when learners have reading fluency or comprehension problems. These learners may or may not have been formally diagnosed as dyslexic. However, they usually are well aware that they have had problems reading since childhood and will tell you that they still have great difficulties saying individual letters and words, as well as understanding the words, either alone, in sentences, or in paragraphs.

The groups of techniques that will be outlined in Chapter 5 include:

- verbal rehearsal or verbal mediation;
- repeated readings;
- adjunct questioning;
- descriptive and sequential organizers;
- the use of such technical equipment as tape recorders and earphones.
- DRTA (Directed Reading and Thinking Activities);
- the ConStruct Procedure;
- Multipass;
- the SQ3R method; and
- ReQuest.

Notetaking and Written Language

The notetaking and written language strategies described in Chapter 6 are intended to help learners write more accurately and more effectively. These techniques include:

- graphic and sequential organizers;
- effective use of microcomputers and tape recorders;
- sentence combining;
- use of a diary;
- Editwrite aids for editing;
- signaling/highlighting.

The Acquisition Process

The first step for instructors who wish to help adults with learning disabilities is to acquire a thorough understanding of the various compensatory and instructional strategies. The second step is to decide which strategies are most appropriate for their learners in either classrooms or one-on-one counseling. The third and crucial step is to learn themselves the most effective way to teach learning disabled individuals how to use and *acquire* the compensatory strategies appropriately.

When informal diagnostic measures have been completed, or a formal assessment report has been obtained, and the adult educator has decided what compensatory strategies might effectively meet the needs of learners, it is not enough, at this point, simply to tell learners what to do. People with learning disabilities, not unlike the rest of us, often do not like to admit that they cannot do something. But, more importantly, they simply will not grasp a strategy by verbal or written instruction alone. They must "experience" the way a technique works. In fact, Schumaker, Deshler, Alley & Warner (1983) state that their research on learning strategies shows that, without specific planned acquisition steps, there will be little, if any, generalization and transference of knowledge or skills. And, generalization is vital if learners are to continue to use a strategy independently long after they have been taught it. In order for students really to learn the strategies, or, in adult education terms, to move them from dependence to self-direction, the strategies and supports must be fully explained, the procedures carefully demonstrated, and enough time allotted for practice. Therefore, when implementing any strategy or introducing any technical device, adult educators can be most effective if they routinely explain, demonstrate, and practice, before learners try to use them.

In order to improve the chances for successful learning and generalization, *six steps*—explanation, modeling, self-instruction, practice, feedback, and implementation—are now briefly outlined. These six steps overlap and are not time-consuming to present. In one-on-one counseling, the steps occur in a back-and-forth interactive flow of learning during one session. In a classroom or training context, demonstration, practice, and feedback can be carried out in one or two class periods.

Step One: Explanation

The adult educator explains in detail what the strategy or aid is, what it is intended to accomplish, and the most effective way to use it. Avoid technical language as much as possible. If informal assessment revealed that learners were visually oriented, show the strategy diagrammatically; if assessment showed an auditory preference, have learners write or print a list of each of the steps involved. On the other hand, if participants learn best by memorization, have them write out and memorize each of the steps involved in the strategy.

Step Two: Modeling

Following the explanation of the strategy, the instructor demonstrates how the strategy is to be used. In the case of learner-based strategies, it is most effective to apply the actual aid or strategy to a current academic task rather than an unconnected demonstration example. People with learning disabilities do not need extra work to do; they frequently need help just doing their required work. An example unrelated to their current needs is apt to have a negative affect on motivation and perseverance.

The following example of modeling and practising concerns a real problem—the difficulty of taking meaningful notes in a class or lecture situation. In this case, special needs counselors can model the columnar format strategy (Chapter 5) by showing the learners a sample, and then by having students take short-form notes while listening to a ten-minute mini-lecture based on students' own course readings.

Or, if modeled and practised during an instructional lesson, educators can show learners how to use the notetaking strategy at the start of an actual class, and then discuss the results at the end of the session. Industrial trainers or literacy tutors can follow a similar process.

Step Three: Self-Instruction

Once the demonstration is completed, instructors should ask learners to explain in their own words the purpose and procedure of the strategy. This provides learners with an opportunity to verbally rehearse what has been learned and shows instructors whether or not their demonstration has been successful. If there is a sensory impairment that makes speech difficult or impossible, learners can demonstrate understanding in some other way (e.g. signing, typing, writing, or drawing).

Step Four: Practice

This step is (or can be) a continuation of the modeling process, but is usually carried out in more detail and depth. Try to use learning materials, assignments, or activities that are current. For example, when learning how to make a flowchart, in preparation for writing an essay, it would be best to base the chart on an actual reading required for the development of that essay. Whatever the aid or strategy, always allow sufficient time for practice.

Step Five: Feedback

During the practice stage, and later, allow time for feedback—both for the learner and the educator. Most adults with learning disabilities have plenty of experience with failure and its attendant criticism. Therefore, for the sake of their self-esteem, give feedback that is affirmative and constructive, such as encouraging learners to reflect on their own performance, or what they think about the strategy. Educators can then respond positively to learner reactions or reflections.

Step Six: Implementation

The final stage occurs when learners use compensatory strategies independently and routinely. For student-related compensatory strategies, usually taught by a counselor or teacher advisor, participants should keep track of any difficulties they may encounter so that, with their instructors, they can discover what aspect of the strategy needs more explanation, modeling, or practice. If more help is needed, go back to the acquisition step that should be re-experienced in order to understand properly and learn the strategy. When learners are able to use a strategy without adult educators' assistance, generalization and self-direction have occurred.

Principles of Adult Learning

No book on adult education is complete without some discussion of the principles of adult learning. Although a complete description is beyond the scope of this book (cf. Brundage and Mackeracher, 1980; Cranton, 1989), it is useful to state the four principles which underlie the concepts in this book.

- *Learning is a lifelong process.* Adult learners need to feel that their previous and current learning experiences have relevance to their present and future lives.
- *Adults learn best when personally involved* in the process of planning, assessment, and implementation in an environment that is not threatening to their self-esteem.
- *Adults prefer and need to learn* how *to learn* so that they can generalize that ability to all learning situations.
- *Adults learn best when they are motivated* to change, undertake a process of self-discovery, or acquire a set of specific skills and strategies.

Summary

The goals of this handbook are to provide adult educators with:

- an informal method to assess the needs of learning disabled adults;
- information on formal assessment procedures that can be used in conjunction with the informal assessment method when a discrepancy identification of learning disabilities is required;
- instructional techniques to be used in their classrooms or other learning settings; and
- strategies to enable learning disabled adults to compensate for their learning deficits.

The next chapter gets the adult educator started. It presents the first steps in the compensatory strategies process: namely, how to find out what learners' difficulties are; when formal testing is appropriate; and how HELP can contribute to decisions on program development.

2
Assessment for Programming

One of the biggest problems currently facing educators in industry or in higher education is programming for their learning disabled students and workers with special needs. Too often, educators have at hand no practical, proven methods of deciding which techniques will be most effective. Trial and error is used to match learning difficulties with compensatory techniques, or, alternatively, a complete formal assessment report with clearly articulated conclusions and educationally-based recommendations is obtained.

The purposes of this chapter are to discuss some formal assessment materials, and to provide the guidance necessary to enable instructors to administer an *informal* assessment, which can be especially helpful when access to formal assessment is neither practical nor available.

The diagnostic tool used to provide informal assessment is called HELP, an acronym for a "Holistic Educational Literacy Process." HELP is intended primarily for use by special needs and assessment counselors or human resource staff, who are able to work one-on-one with individuals. However, in addition, both educational instructors and industrial trainers can easily use HELP informally to assess their students or personnel. Use of or exposure to this test procedure can also increase understanding of potential problems in the skills areas covered, give a more informed basis on which to make referrals for formal assessment, and improve understanding and use of diagnostic reports.

The eight steps of this test can be administered in approximately an hour and a half, and an additional hour or so is required to draw up conclusions and recommendations for programming.

The diagnostic procedures of the process are intended to improve programming in literacy-related skills only, such as reading fluency, comprehension, oral communication, thinking, memory, and written language, rather than, for example, to analyze psychologically-based difficulties, such as inappropriate social skills. Thus, the assessment tool will provide a basis for developing a compensatory adult education program, as opposed to suggesting directions for psychological counseling, or attempting to isolate neurological or biochemical factors.

First, formal assessment methods are briefly described. It is helpful to have some knowledge of these methods when using psychoeducational reports as the basis for program decisions and modifications. In addition, examples of formal measures that can be used to pinpoint specific learning disabilities will be presented after the informal HELP approach has been outlined.

Formal Assessment

Formal assessments are standardized tests, i.e. tests which have been compiled empirically, have definite directions for administration and use, have adequate norms, and have data on reliability and validity. The purpose of a formal assessment is twofold: to establish if there is a discrepancy between intellectual potential and actual, current functioning, and to exclude other possible problems as the primary cause of the discrepancy.

Formal assessments are carried out by professionals trained in the administration of tests and diagnosis of learning disabilities, or by individuals working under the supervision of such professionals. While other, more general, educational test measures can be carried out by someone with special training, adult educators should not attempt to administer any formal assessment without the supervision of someone trained to conduct such procedures and interpret the results. However, adult educators can use any available formal reports as a further aid to understanding students' learning problems, in addition to the HELP assessment process.

Readers may find helpful the following outline of some formal tests and what their subtests measure. (For a complete list of test instruments and publishers of list materials, see either Johnson and Blalock 1987a, Appendices D & E or Swanson and Watson, 1982.)

- The *Wechsler Adult Intelligence Scale,* better known simply as the WAIS, is the most widely used intelligence test for adults. This series should *only* be administered by a registered psychologist or one who has the specialized training to do so.
- The *Detroit Tests of Learning Aptitude* (DTLA-2) helps pinpoint learning aptitudes in literacy-related areas. Especially useful are the subtests on oral directions, word sequences, story construction, object and letter sequences, design reproduction, and word fragments (visual closure).
- The *Stanford Diagnostic Reading Test* (SDRT) contains subtests on auditory vocabulary, reading comprehension, and phonetic analysis (being able to identify and use sounds appropriately). The usual adult performance levels are brown or blue, Form A.
- The *Learning Efficiency Test* (LET) provides information about visual and auditory memory strengths and weaknesses in immediate, short-term, and long-term recall and retrieval; namely, SM, STM and LTM.
- The *Slosson Oral Reading Test* (SORT) and the *Diagnostic Screening Test* (DST) help identify whether the person learns and remembers words using a phonics or whole-word approach. The tests also give some indication of ability to spell.
- The *Test of Written Language* (TOWL-2), especially the subtests on vocabulary and word usage, thematic maturity (age appropriate topics), are useful to find out learners' familiarity with rules usage, punctuation, and capitalization.
- The *California Verbal Learning Test*—Adult Version (C-V-L-T) is an excellent predictor of individual memory capacity and to what extent the participant already uses strategies.
- The *Wide Range Achievement Test* (WRAT-R, Adult) tests spelling, reading, and arithmetic, and is a valuable tool in determining a learning disability. It is designed to eliminate, as much as possible, the effects of cultural bias.
- The *Spadafore Diagnostic Reading Test* (SDRT) can help to determine literacy levels, using subtests that profile silent reading and listening comprehension performance.

Faculty and staff frequently refer students or personnel for formal assessment in order to help decide whether they have the intellectual ability to handle course content or meet job requirements. Formal assessment can determine whether a learning disability diagnosis is appropriate. To do this, it must be demonstrated that a "discrepancy" exists between learners' potential ability and their demonstrated achievement. It must also be established that the discrepancy is *not* primarily due to intellectual, emotional, physical, or cultural factors (cf. Bachor & Crealock, 1986,17).

When formal assessment does reveal such a "discrepancy," there is evidence of a broad variation between one area of learning and another. For example, if learners have high performance equivalents in reading comprehension and low performance equivalents in reading fluency, they may be classic dyslexics. They probably have great difficulty with decoding, meaning access, and sentence integration, but they may be better at making inferences (due to life experiences) and using contextual cues to monitor and comprehend the reading material in the test (Mayer, 1987).

Both formal, as well as informal testing, should be conducted in the following four instances:

- if, during the preliminary interview process, a history of extensive learning disabilities is uncovered;
- if, during the first steps of HELP, learners are simply not able to complete the process because of a lack of skills and abilities;
- if, at the conclusion of HELP, the tester is unable to come up with a hypothesis as to which compensatory strategies will help learners; or,
- if a formal diagnosis of a learning disability is required.

However, formal assessment procedures, which are costly and time-consuming, are not essential in most cases. Although informal measures cannot generate a formal label of learning disabilities, they can reveal discrepancies and provide useful information. Using interview techniques, the oral or written input of instructors, and the diagnostic tool HELP, invaluable information can be gained to help answer the learning needs of students.

Informal Assessment

Adult educators conduct informal assessments every time they talk to learners. Whether conscious of what they are doing or not, instructors make frequent educational judgements on the basis of what students say. The first step in any informal assessment process should be an introductory interview, which can uncover learners' family and educational histories, occupational backgrounds and aspirations, and current learning problems. Some learners know a great deal about their difficulties; others know only that it is difficult to complete course readings and assignments at an acceptable level.

A major barrier to understanding is that a learning disability is *invisible* to everyone. It only manifests itself in the work learning disabled individuals cannot do. Michaels (1986, 79) states that there is a lack of understanding of literacy-related problems on the part of faculty members of many community colleges. A common questions is: "If students can't read or can't write adequately what are they doing in a regular college?"

This situation, in which both instructor and student cannot "see" the problem but notice its results, leads to low learner self-esteem and frustration with poor motivation and perseverance. Individuals with learning disabilities are often most fearful of the very people who can help them. This insecurity and sensitivity often emerges during the informal interview process. More than one session may be needed in order to break down the barriers erected by learners to hide their learning or functioning difficulties. Time taken to develop rapport during the initial interview(s) will be well rewarded with valuable informal assessment information.

Once the interview is complete and an initial hypothesis made, tell learners what their learning problems may be. In fact, to ease anxiety, learners should be kept informed at every step of the assessment process. Moreover, they have lived with their difficulties for a long time, and although they may not have the technical vocabulary to articulate their problems, they can offer information that often proves valuable for diagnosis and remediation. For example, some students may reveal that they just can't seem to understand when reading silently or reading something for the first time; this is an indication that they can probably benefit from verbal rehearsal or a repeated reading strategy. When administering HELP to such learners, pay close attention to how well they do during the oral reading, listening, and notetaking steps to see if the repetitive nature of the process helps comprehension. It usually does!

After the interview(s) are completed, educators and learners are ready to begin the informal testing process using HELP.

HELP For Informal Assessment

When formal testing measures are not indicated or not possible, informal assessment is a realistic alternative. The specific informal assessment tool, HELP, was developed for two main purposes:

- to meet the need for an informal assessment tool, as the first step in the programming process, for the increasing numbers of learning disabled people in adult education classrooms and occupational settings;
- to provide a preliminary diagnostic tool to determine whether formal testing is necessary, and if so, which tests should be used after completion of HELP.

Description

A whole language approach was chosen as the framework for HELP in order to give adult educators a "whole picture" of which skills and cognitive processes learners have at their disposal in everyday occupational or learning settings. A whole language model for the assessment and diagnosis of literacy and learning deficits also ensures a multidimensional approach that not only involves speaking, listening, reading, and writing, but also involves the use of various audiovisual aids and organizers.

Hollingsworth and Reutzel (1988) originally suggested this model for children, but its methods and framework have been adapted here for adult learners. This test is activity-based, involves learner input, and engages participants in typical language transactions rather than isolated instructional drills and formal subtests.

Although HELP can be modified for use with learning disabled individuals with sensory impairments, the model described, as it is now used, was designed and developed for learners who can use these senses at least to a minimal degree.

The whole language base and step-by-step nature of HELP make it compatible with such principles of instructional design as proceeding from simple to complex, concrete to abstract, and known to unknown (Kemp, 1985). Task analysis is facilitated as each step of the procedure breaks down various literacy and thinking processes into small chunks so as to help adult educators and their learners more easily identify learning problems.

Gagne (1987, 141) states that educators must: (1) break down the learning and teaching process into bite-sized chunks; (2) determine which chunks are most important; (3) decide which should be taught first; and (4) understand how they are related to one another. Administering HELP will help educators begin that process.

Because HELP is informal, educators will *not* need to know or use technical vocabulary. (Formal terminology will be used in this handbook to describe or discuss the HELP steps only when necessary.) All that is needed is the ability to observe, ask questions, and record observations and best guesses about particular problem areas being tested.

It is easiest to use a booklet format to take notes for later examination and reflection. For example, a set of sheets with preprinted headings for each of the eight steps in HELP can be created. However, some steps require the use of large chart paper. Be sure to record how learners react to the task and the skills that were or were not apparent during the test. All these notes will be necessary in order to make concrete decisions when developing a compensatory strategies program.

Each of the HELP steps will now be outlined under the following headings:

- the *process* involved in each step, i.e. how the procedures within each step are conducted;
- the *purpose* of the step and what research says about the importance of each procedure within that step;

- a helpful list of *results indicating problems,* following each step;
- *examples of results* which might occur and might be used as the basis for program planning. These examples are intended to provide additional information only and should not be used as the basis for an identification of a discrepancy indicating a learning disability; that diagnosis can only be made following a formal assessment. Some people may exhibit some of the learning problems listed but do not necessarily have learning disabilities;
- examples of *possible formal tests* that could be used in conjunction with HELP. However, the entire HELP procedure should be finished before administering any formal methods, in keeping with the whole language feature of HELP; and
- *where to find appropriate strategies* in this book to compensate for the learning problems uncovered.

Readers are encouraged to refer to Figures 2–1, 2–2, and 2–3 for clarification of the process.

Guide to Using Figures 2–1 and 2–3

Figure 2–1

Each of the tasks required in the eight steps of HELP is identified in Figure 2–1. The literacy-related task required for each step is listed immediately under the step number and task required. For example, the "task" required for Step One is to "read aloud into a tape recorder."

The literacy skills or strategies being evaluated informally are listed down the *left* column and are shown under each step as the *shaded* areas. Because of the *interconnectedness* of the whole language approach of the HELP procedure, several skills are assessed in each step of HELP.

Figure 2–3

Should formal assessment measures be needed, once the entire HELP procedure is completed, examples of the kinds of instruments that could be used are identified under each step. For example, if more information is required on the task done in Step One (see Figure 2–1), oral reading, the Wide Range Achievement Test Reading Subtest (WRAT-R, Adult) can be used, as well as the Diagnostic Screening Test (DST). (See the formal assessment section in this chapter for a brief explanation for each of the formal test examples.) An

Figure 2-1: The HELP Informal Assessment Steps

INFORMAL ASSESSMENT TASK / Literacy Skills/Strategies Needed	Step 1 — Read Aloud Into Tape Recorder	Step 2 — Listen With Earphones	Step 3 — Listen Again and Take Notes	Step 4 — Highlight Main Points (Signaling)	Step 5 — Develop An Organizing Structure	Step 6 — Write A Short Summary	Step 7 — Review And Revise Summary	Step 8 — Reflect on Summary and Discuss Conclusions
THINKING • abstract reasoning • problem solving • strategy learning • building internal and external connections • critical reflection • attention span (working memory) • visual spatial abilities			■	■	■	■		■
ORAL COMMUNICATION • receptive (perception, comprehension, memory) • expressive (retrieval, vocabulary rule usage, pronunciation & sequencing ideas/concepts)	■	■	■		■			
READING • auditory language (saying the words subvocally) • verbal processing • context association • comprehension/content analysis • spelling (decoding/phonics analysis)	■			■	■	■	■	■
WRITTEN LANGUAGE • composition/sentence construction • revision (self-monitoring) • organization • handwriting • punctuation, capitalization			■	■	■	■	■	

Strategies needed = ■
Strategies not needed = ☐

estimate of the time required for both HELP and the formal procedures is
listed under each step.

Step One: Oral Reading

The Process

Participants choose a passage of text on a topic that interests them but
which they have *not* read before. They need only read the text, or a portion
of it, for a period of from five to ten minutes. If learners have difficulty with
the text selection process, counselors can help them locate something that is
of interest and at the appropriate reading level. If learners are in an educational or industrial setting, recommend that they use one of their course- or
work-related readings.

The chosen passage is read into a tape recorder at a pace determined by
the learners. If necessary, before starting, learners are taught how to use the
stop/start buttons on the equipment. Although the learners will be questioned
on the content of this material when finished, they should be told to concentrate on reading the words accurately. The rationale for this is the *focal
attention hypothesis,* that for fluency, concentration should be placed on the
printed words themselves, rather than on context and comprehension which
can be distracting (Mayer, 1987, 261).

The Purpose

The purpose of this step is twofold: to discover if readers have (1) reading
fluency and/or (2) comprehension difficulties. In the first instance, to detect
fluency problems, adult educators must listen carefully to the way the reader
reads. Only later, when comprehension questions are asked, will it become
obvious how much meaning was accessed and processed.

Reading fluency is a separate area of assessment and consists of decoding
(the process of translating a printed word into sounds), accessing meaning
(determining a word's meaning in a particular sentence) and sentence integration (being able to combine meanings of all the individual words into a
complete sentence).

Reading comprehension, assessed after the oral reading is completed,
involves finding out to what extent the readers understood the reading pas-

sage. To be able to comprehend material, learners must be able to access any prior knowledge of the topic of the reading, remember information, make inferences, and use contextual cues and monitoring techniques (Mayer, 1987 and Wolf, 1984).

Language, like other areas of learning, must be examined in relation to learners' backgrounds, educational levels, and academic skills. This is particularly important when assessing adults whose daily experiences are more varied than those of children.

Figure 2–1, Step One, reveals that the process of oral reading involves many skills and strategies. It is no wonder that some individuals find reading aloud laborious and comprehension monitoring difficult, especially since all of the fluency skills first must be automatic in order to be able to utilize the more abstract comprehension skills. Fluent readers are so practised in word recognition and decoding that they are unaware of these processes; instead, fluent readers concentrate on monitoring the meaning of what they are reading. The assumption is, therefore, that if people have great difficulty with the reading in Step One, they may have problems with the same skills in which the fluent reader excels—both fluency and comprehension.

Compared to those who read effortlessly, people who have difficulty reading may have: (1) smaller vocabularies; (2) less exposure to complex sentences; and (3) less general information (Blalock, 1987, 82). Thus, people can find reading orally difficult for many reasons, some of which already may have been uncovered during the preliminary interview process.

Results Indicating Problems in Oral Reading

Reading Fluency

- inability to sound out words, i.e. difficulty associating sounds with letters;
- poor sight vocabulary and word identification, i.e. difficulty recognizing many words (related problems in spelling are frequent);
- generally inaccurate reading;
- mispronunciation;
- transposition of letters in words;
- tendency to repeat words;
- skipping words or whole lines (may indicate problems with comprehending syntax);

- frequently losing place;
- hesitation when reading;
- reading very slowly;
- being unaware of errors or problems.

Comprehension

- inability to understand meaning of a passage on first reading;
- inability to find the main idea of the passage on a first reading;
- difficulty making inferences on first reading;
- little or no spontaneous or automatic use of context clues;
- inability to use and build on prior knowledge;
- inability to monitor whether material is understood.

Examples of Results

People who find Step One difficult will either read with frequent hesitations, repetitions, substitutions, omissions, incorrect pronunciation, poor word recognition skills, and/or an inability to sound out and identify certain words; or, not remember anything about the passage just read. Although learners are told to concentrate only on fluency, they do know that they will be asked some questions on content. A complete lack of recall would suggest that they have been totally absorbed in trying to figure out what the words say and mean.

These informal findings can be indicators of problems in the two areas of skills processing needed for reading orally; namely, accuracy in decoding and comprehension monitoring.

For fluency, the skills of decoding, meaning access, and sentence integration are required. For comprehension, readers must be able to make inferences, connect incoming information with that already in long-term memory, use context clues, and monitor whether they understand the reading material. "Classic" dyslexics have difficulty with fluency, although they are often able to compensate for such deficits with strong contextual comprehension strategies. However, in order to be a fluent reader in every sense, skills in both processing areas are required.

Figure 2-2: Imagery Organizer of HELP Steps

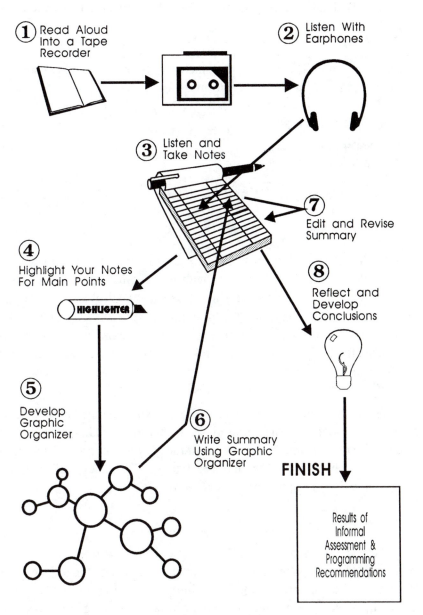

Possible Formal Tests

In cases where problems are uncovered by Step One, formal tests can be used to investigate further. Two possible formal tests are indicated on Figure 2-3 (other useful tests are also available).

- The Wide Range Achievement Test—Revised (WRAT-R) Reading Subtest;
- The Diagnostic Screening Test (DST).

Figure 2-3 also indicates the approximate time required to administer the HELP steps and these supplementary formal tests.

Where to Find Strategies

- Chapter 5
- Figure 5-1 (examples)

Step Two: Listen With Earphones

The Process

During this step, participants listen to the passage they previously recorded, *while wearing earphones.* As with the tape-recording process, the earphones allow participants a measure of personal control as they are free to operate the recorder themselves. In addition, only the learners actually listen to their own reading, thus reducing any embarrassment if they experienced difficulty in Step One. The earphones also seem to keep external distractions to a minimum.

When participants are finished listening, ask them what they now remember about the passage that they did not remember after reading aloud. Most subjects will now remember something. In fact, many will process meaning automatically, while listening, without realizing it. Write down all they say that might help in later programming decisions.

The Purpose

Step Two is designed to provide information on how well students can listen. Educators are aware of the vital link between being able to listen and being able to process information. The ability to listen effectively is not a single skill; most thinking, memory, and abstract reasoning processes are involved. Blalock (1987, 92) states that "retaining an appropriate amount of

Figure 2-3: Examples of Formal Assessment After HELP

INFORMAL ASSESSMENT TASK	Step 1 Read Aloud Into Tape Recorder	Step 2 Listen With Earphones	Step 3 Listen Again and Take Notes	Step 4 Highlight Main Points (Signaling)	Step 5 Develop An Organizing Structure	Step 6 Write A Short Summary	Step 7 Review and Revise Summary	Step 8 Reflect On Summary and Discuss Conclusions
EXAMPLES OF FORMAL ASSESSMENT MEASURES *	WRAT-R Reading Subtest, *and* DST Spelling: Phonics/ whole word decoding & word recognition	C-V-L-T Adult: Listening & Memory Strategy Usage (3 Trials) *or* SDRT Listening Comprehension	DTLA-2 Subtest III Oral Directions	DTLA-2 Subtest X Word Fragments *and* DTLA-2 Subtest VII Object Sequences *and* DTLA-2 Subtest IX Letter Sequences	LET Visual & Auditory Memory Learning Style *and* DTLA-2 Subtest VI Design Reproduction	TOWL-2 Subtest 4 Logical Sentences & Word Usage	TOWL-2 Subtest 5 Sentence Combining, Punctuation & Capitalization	DTLA-2 Subtest VIII Symbolic Relations *and/or* DTLA-2 Subtest V Story Construction
Approximate Time Required (in minutes):								
HELP: 90	10	10	15	10	10	15	10	10
Formal: 100	15	15	10	15	15	10	10	10
Totals: 190 (about 3 hours)	25	25	25	25	25	25	20	20

*Based on the results of the *completed* HELP procedure. For a brief description of these formal tests see page 19.

auditory information in the correct sequence long enough to act on it, repeat it, or commit it to intermediate or long-term memory is an important auditory 'receptive' ability." Because of the complexity of the listening process many learning disabled students have trouble remembering what they hear.

Listening to one's own voice does, of course, involve hearing one's own speech patterns. However, if listeners' speech patterns are incorrect, they can learn from their mistakes. Although some professionals think that listening to one's own speech deficits only reinforces those errors, this need not be the case. Ochs and Schieffelin (1979) find that effective listening requires competency in oral language. And in turn, the process of listening itself strengthens such skills as deriving meaning from contextual cues, recalling words, correct pronunciation, and vocabulary expansion (Kuhl 1982).

Results Indicating Problems in Auditory Processing

Listening

- inability to retain information presented orally;
- problems understanding and following spoken directions or instructions;
- understanding less when listening than when reading;
- inability to take notes in class situations;
- difficulty discriminating sounds in words;
- confusing similar sounds;
- speech inaccuracies.

Examples of Results

Some learners will report that they were unable to concentrate on what they were saying and could catch only the odd sentence. If so, they may have problems with auditory discrimination, or nonverbal reasoning strategies such as little or no access to verbal labels or verbal rehearsal strategies (Johnson and Blalock, 1987b). Listening problems, revealed through informal assessment, can indicate difficulties in deriving meaning from contextual cues, recalling words, proper pronunciation, and vocabulary.

Possible Formal Tests

In cases where problems are uncovered by Step Two, formal tests can be used to investigate further. Two possible formal tests are indicated on Figure 2-3.

- The California Verbal Inventory Test (C-V-L-T.) is useful for determining ability to recall and the strategies used by the listener.
- The Stanford Diagnostic Reading Test (SDRT) can be used to pinpoint severe difficulties with listening comprehension.

Where to Find Strategies

- Chapter 5
- Figure 5-1 (examples)

Step Three: Listening and Notetaking

The Process

Step Three involves listening a second time to the learner's tape-recorded passage, with earphones, while simultaneously taking short-form notes. Participants are to write only what they think is essential. Suggest that they pretend they are writing the notes for readers who need to know what the reading was about, but don't have time to read it themselves. Before beginning, it is again important that educators make sure that learners have understood the instructions, and that they know how to start and stop the tape recorder at any time.

There are many notetaking formats; recommended is a page divided into three sections (see Figure 2–4, a modification of what is presented in Chapter 6 and that used by Alley and Deshler (1979) in their book on learning strategies for adolescents.) In HELP, the largest section, the left half of the page, is used to take short-form notes. The top right-hand section is used for writing and revising a summary of the notes taken. The bottom section is for reflections and conclusions based on the summary. (These components will be explained later in Steps Six to Eight.)

The Purpose

During the process of taking notes, underlying problems in areas such as comprehension and organizing thoughts logically may be uncovered. In order to complete this task successfully, learners must have the ability to listen, comprehend, synthesize, and extract main ideas simultaneously, and then retain them long enough to formulate and write a synopsis. In addition, the motor act of writing requires automaticity and speed in letter formation, and the resulting handwriting must be sufficiently legible for others to read (Vogel, 1987, 253). Spelling must also be accurate. Taking notes in lectures is a high level task which many learning disabled people find extremely difficult.

Unfortunately, notetaking often is considered a waste of time for those students who cannot do it easily. However, Mayer (1987, 199) states that, to the contrary, it is not a minor chore with little benefit to learners; rather, the notetaking process can have great impact on the transfer of knowledge. This transference occurs more readily because notetaking acts as an organizer in guiding attention and connecting new information to what is already known.

Results Indicating Problems in Notetaking

* agitation and frustration revealed while performing the task;
* indecision about what to include in notes;
* attempts made to write everything down;
* inability to identify main ideas;
* inability to distinguish supporting detail;
* inability to remember what has been said long enough to make note of it;
* slow writing.

Examples of Results

Despite its complexity, all learners who proceed this far in the informal diagnostic process are able to take notes to some extent. Although a typical comment is, "I usually don't remember enough to be able to write notes," it is probable that they have been able to process more meaning from the reading material during the test because of the repetition provided by the successive HELP steps and the use of the tape recorder (Vogel, 1987). However, their notes may be sloppy, brief, confused, disorganized, missing vital information, lacking in detail, and may include irrelevant or erroneous detail.

Difficulties in this step of the test can tell adult educators a great deal about the learning needs of students. However, it may be necessary to ask many questions to uncover underlying factors in a particular problem area. For example, learners may have difficulties with concentration or memory processing. Problems in detecting main ideas may be due to difficulty in deciding which are the important points, an inability to organize and connect thoughts, a memory deficiency, problems with auditory discrimination, or a combination of any of the above.

Possible Formal Tests

The essence of Step Three is to determine whether learners can listen and write simultaneously. A formal test is indicated on Figure 2-3.

- The Detroit Tests of Learning Aptitude (DTLA-2), Subtest III, "oral directions," is a very telling formal measure.

Where to Find Strategies

- Chapter 5
- Figure 5-1 (examples)
- Chapter 6
- Figures 6-1, 6-4, 6-5 (examples)

Step Four: Signaling

The Process

During this step, learners look over the short-form notes taken in Step Three, and then highlight the *most* important and relevant points to help in both recall and organization. These may be single words, phrases, or entire sentences. Signaling may be done by underlining or by using a colored, transparent, highlighting accent marker.

If learners are unable to perform the task, e.g. they are unable to identify the signals (clues) or the major points, ask them to discuss the meaning of the passage. Once readers are able to produce appropriate potential notes orally, ask them to go back and accent or underline only those words and phrases that are most important. If they still are unable to perform this task, it is evident that they have trouble synthesizing what they read and hear.

The Purpose

Assuming that the information learners have written in their short-form notes during the previous step of the test is accurate, the purposes of the signaling task is to indicate whether or not learners know how to: (1) direct their attention to the main ideas; (2) see how one part of a reading passage is connected to another (Mayer, 1987, 193); and (3) relate new information to what they already know about the topic. Signaling, like notetaking, involves much more than simply picking out words in an aimless fashion; difficulties in performing the task reveal weaknesses in learners' thought processes.

And, as well as a testing tool, it is an excellent compensatory technique to help learners acquire the skills discussed above.

Signaling is an example of a generative technique, aimed at improving reading comprehension by connecting old knowledge, that information already held in the memory, with new incoming knowledge (Mayer, 1987). It is a technique to build on what is already known and stresses the importance of the new material. Signaling is a strategy that both guides attention and organizes relevant information.

People who use generative techniques automatically are more effective readers, notetakers, and writers. Some researchers have found that students who actively organize a lecture into an outline can recall more than those who did not take notes, even when the notetaking students were not given an opportunity to review the notes they had written (Barnett, DiVesta & Rogozinski, 1981).

Results Indicating Problems in Signaling

- unwillingness to try or inability to complete the task;
- indecision about what to include;
- original notes too sparse;
- inability to identify some or all of the main ideas;
- inability to identify supporting detail;
- difficulty connecting one part of a reading passage to another, e.g. seeing cause and effect;
- inability to relate the new ideas to what is already known about the topic;
- overuse of highlighting.

Examples of Results

Some adult learners, who do fairly well during the notetaking step, can also highlight (signal) without much difficulty. Even if they failed to take effective notes in Step Four, they will not necessarily have difficulty with this signaling task. Learners can suddenly remember information they previously forgot. They often understand much more than they were able to record. Some do not do well under pressure and may need time to go back and reexamine what they wrote. If so, they should be allowed to go back to the previous stage and fill in more notes.

Figure 2-4: Three Column Format for HELP	
Notetaking and Highlighting: Steps 3 and 4	**Summary and Revision: Steps 6 and 7**
	Reflections and Conclusions: Step 8

But, many people with learning disabilities may highlight almost everything or almost nothing. They seem to have great difficulty deciding which ideas are most important and, as a result, have problems prioritizing what they have read when required to organize and write a summary. They need to know how to find the main ideas and how to distinguish them from secondary points, and to be able to understand relationships among ideas. Problems at this point may indicate learners have difficulties understanding what they read and therefore cannot properly integrate words and sentences into coherent concepts. Including this step in HELP aids in assessing learners' abilities in these areas.

These generative or reading comprehension deficits will probably lead to continual failure, because most tasks in further education or work involve reading, notetaking, and writing, and the ability to generate or identify ideas.

Learners also need to be able to make connections between new information and what is already known. People with learning problems in these areas can improve with the use of compensatory strategies, as outlined in Chapters 5 and 6, that help them organize and integrate their thinking and writing processes. However, it may be necessary to recommend formal assessment if some improvement is not noted soon.

At this point in the administration of HELP, adult learners have been involved in all of the whole language processes. From here to the end of HELP, each of those processes will be reinforced. Although oral communication is not identified in Figure 2–1 for each of the final steps, learners and adult educators are involved in continuous feedback and discussion.

Possible Formal Tests

The following formal subtests can be useful to clarify problems in this area, as indicated on Figure 2-3:

- The Detroit Tests of Learning Aptitude (DTLA-2), Subtests X, "Word Fragments," VII, "Object Sequences," and IX, "Letter Sequences."

Where to Find Strategies

- Chapters 3 and 6
- Figures 3-1, 3-2, and 6-1 (examples)

Step Five: Pictorial and Other Organizers

The Process

In Step Five learners must perform a task that requires at least some ability in abstract reasoning skills (see Figure 2–1). Based on their highlighted notes (signals), participants are asked to devise a visual or sequential organizer, (a method of recording information in a picture, chart, list, etc.). This may take the form of an imagery map, an itemized list, or a conceptual diagram (see Figures 2–2, 2–5, and 2–6). Figures 2–2, an imagery organizer, and 2–5, a bubble flowchart, are models that are usually preferred by people who have a visual learning style and prefer to "see" what they learn. The chart in Figure 2–6 is an organizer that may be preferred by those with an auditory learning style because of its sequential nature. (For a complete definition of learning styles see Chapter 1.)

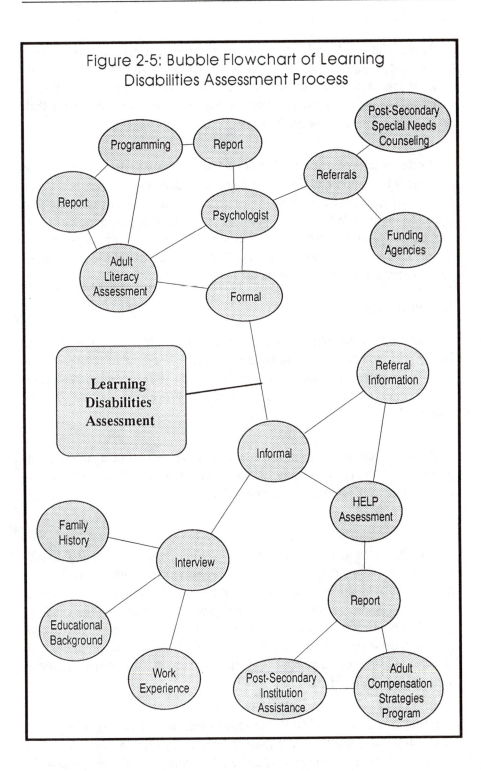

Figure 2-5: Bubble Flowchart of Learning Disabilities Assessment Process

Demonstrate and explain various types of organizers and ask learners which one they prefer to use. If they have trouble with the one they first choose, substitute one that has different processing requirements. Participants may have been using strategies that are not compatible with their learning style preferences and strengths.

Whatever style of organizer is selected, learners are to design it to include only the information highlighted in Step Four. Once the diagram is finished have students explain, in detail, what their structure means and why it is organized as it is. While any paper may be used, large primary chart paper can be hung on the wall when it is time for participants' explanations. Supply colored, water-based markers if learners want to color-code or make some information or points more obvious than others.

The Purpose

Most adults with learning disabilities have great difficulty with this task. People who do not have the skills to complete this step often have problems organizing everything else in their lives, especially their own time and responsibilities. In the words of one learner, "I just can't seem to get it all together."

Therefore, the purpose for including the development of a structural organizer in HELP, is to discover, in a very concrete way, how well students can think through an idea, event, or problem.

The importance of being able to organize ideas cannot be underestimated in any adult learning or counseling setting. When people are required to take notes, write exams, prepare presentations, and write essays or reports, they must be able to draw up hypotheses, recommendations, and conclusions. Frequently, learners with organizational problems are among the brightest participants. Unfortunately, as Johnson and Blalock (1987, 1987b, 280) point out, these individuals are usually not able to perform up to their potential because of poor planning ability and an inability to prioritize activities and complete assignments.

Holley and Dansereau (1984) examined the validity of "organizer structures," and found that they contribute to learning by forcing students to build internal and external connections and explanations of a reading passage, as

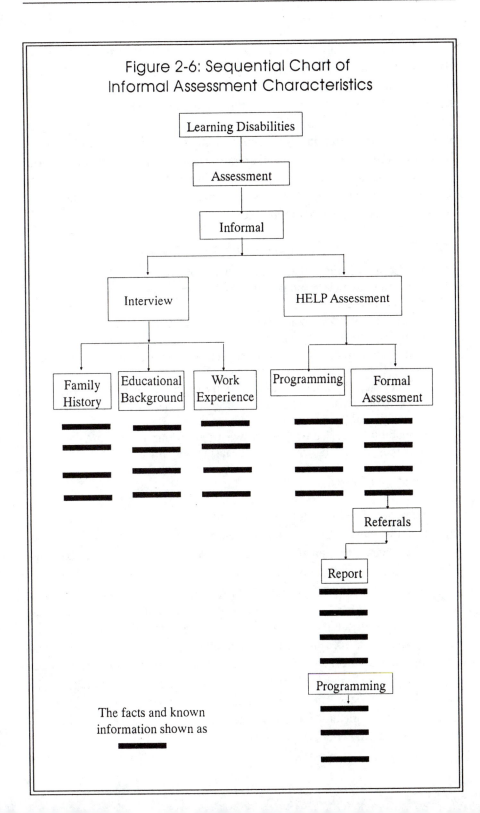

Figure 2-6: Sequential Chart of
Informal Assessment Characteristics

opposed to notetaking and signaling alone, which simply isolate information. Actually, just as with notetaking and signaling, this method is useful when the goal of instruction is to help learners determine what is important versus what is not important in expository material or projects (Mayer, 1987, 191). Therefore, Steps Three, Four, and Five of HELP involve the ability to process new information and connect it to existing knowledge already learned and/or memorized. Another purpose of Step Five is to find out whether participants are most productive using auditory, successive learning processes, such as sequential lists and diagrams, or simultaneous visual processes, as evidenced in a preference for visual or sequential organizers.

Results Indicating Problems with Organizational Skills

- reports by learners that they are always disorganized;
- inability to understand the task at all;
- refusal to undertake the task;
- difficulty knowing which type of organizer to use;
- difficulty prioritizing information;
- trouble making connections between what is highlighted and what should be included in the organizer;
- indecision about what to include in the organizer, where, and why;
- difficulty trying to explain the organizer, due to a lack of understanding of the relationships between the ideas;
- inability to decide or describe what the organizer means, (e.g. what is most important versus what is least important).

Examples of Results

Some people need very little prodding to get started. However, for others, who have difficulty creating ways of presenting information in such a structure, or who cannot organize ideas, start by suggesting that they make a list of the important points. Ask them first to prioritize that list and then place the information on their first item on a large sheet of paper. They now have to choose where to put this information. If they have trouble deciding, suggest the middle of the page. Continue in this way until all the points are on the chart, and then ask learners to connect all the points. As with people who make up their own organizers, individuals must then explain why they put their points where they did, and what it all means in the context of the material read in Step One. When adult learners need such individualized guidance, educators quickly realize that they will need help to organize every step of a project or assignment.

Possible Formal Tests

The following two tests, as indicated on Figure 2-3, provide more information on visual and auditory memory, cognitive learning style, and organizational ability.

- The Learning Efficiency Test (LET)
- The Detroit Tests of Learning Aptitude (DTLA-2), Subtest VI, "Design Reproduction"

Where to Find Strategies

- Chapters 3, 4, 5, and 6
- Figures 2-2, 2-5, 2-6, 3-1, 4-1, 5-1, 5-2, and 6-2 (examples)

Steps Six and Seven: Summarizing and Revising

The Process

The tasks of Steps Six and Seven, writing and revising, represent the culmination of the whole language process. (These two activities require many skills and abilities—see Figure 2–1.) Based on the visual or graphic organizer developed during the previous test step, participants write a short summary, using proper sentence structure. The summary does not have to be more than a few sentences, but must present all the ideas in a logical sequence.

Once the summary is finished, participants read over their own work and see if they can find any errors or omissions. If they are able to self-monitor successfully, they make the appropriate corrections.

Purpose

The purposes of these steps (see Figures 2–1 and 2–4) are to find out if learners can generate and synthesize ideas in a written format, and if they are able to monitor their own writing for errors. The tests are designed to find out how much participants really understand and remember of what they have read, and to what extent they have difficulty with written language, with sentence formation, vocabulary, spelling, or punctuation. In short, can the learners write, or are they functionally illiterate?

Writing is one of the most basic tasks in school and at work. If individuals are unable to express themselves properly in written form, no matter how well they can organize information they will not succeed. Their opportunities will be limited to non-writing positions, of which there are now very few.

Johnson and Blalock (1987b, 279–280) find that many learning disabled adults, even those with good oral language abilities, do not have the written language skills necessary to vary sentences, to summarize, to outline, or to reorganize what they write. They also tend to reverse letters, or portions of letters, and use a mixture of manuscript and cursive lettering in the same written summary.

Results Indicating Problems in Summarizing/Revising

Summarizing

- inability to summarize from organizer chart;
- not knowing how or where to begin;
- inability to identify the main ideas;
- inability to separate main ideas from supporting detail;
- inability to see connections between ideas;
- poor grammar;
- use of sentence fragments;
- difficulty varying sentence structure;
- sentences in an illogical sequence;
- many spelling errors;
- very slow writing;
- illegible writing;
- writing off the lines;
- difficulty copying letters or words;
- tendency to reverse letters or portions of letters;
- writes and prints in the same assignment (mixes scripts);
- responds poorly to pressure.

Revising

- difficulty when asked to scan or discuss what is written;
- difficulty identifying errors in own writing;
- inability to use a dictionary successfully to check for errors;
- different spelling of the same word;
- inability to understand or use grammatically correct sentence structures;
- omission of capital letters and punctuation and inability to identify the correct form.

Examples of Results

Some students do fairly well on all other tasks before writing and revising in Steps Six and Seven. Had a decision been made about their performance on the basis of how well they read, understood what they read, and organized what they read, it probably would have been mistaken. Many of these students produce writing which lacks proper sentence structure, capitalization, or punctuation. When questioned, these same learners cannot decide how to put their thoughts and ideas together in formal expository writing.

Possible Formal Instruments

- The Test of Written Language (TOWL-2), Subtest 4, "Logical Sentences/Word Usage" and Subtest 5, "Sentence Combining, Punctuation, and Capitalization"

Where to Find Strategies

- Chapter 6
- Figures 6-1 (examples)

Step Eight: Abstract Reasoning and Developing Conclusions

The Process

The final step in HELP provides an opportunity for reflection on what was written and revised during Steps Six and Seven. Learners must now try to go beyond what they read and summarized to reason and to think abstractly. This can be tested by returning to the graphic organizers and asking learners to make judgements on the content of the passage read or see its implications. Space is provided in the bottom right section of Figure 2–4 for the learners to write a brief statement of their conclusions.

Essentially, this final step uncovers whether or not adult learners can think critically about what they read and summarized. Can they, for example, discuss what may be implicit in the reading passage?

The Purpose

The ability to think abstractly is part of human intellectual development. Since HELP is designed for adults, it is important to discover whether or not adult learners have reached the formal operations stage of development, which involves a variety of abstract reasoning capacities. Normally, the onset of abstract reasoning marks the beginning of a period in which the transition to adult forms of thought nears completion (Case, 1985, 5). Stone (1987, 67) states that being able to identify and solve problems indicates that individuals have developed the cognitive structures characteristic of formal operational thinking. The purpose of this final step is to observe whether or not learners have made the transition from concrete operations to abstract thinking.

Research on abstract reasoning is scarce. Even the formal assessment instrument mentioned earlier, the WAIS, does not test this capacity. Stone used a variety of assessment methods, in combination with a series of tasks which involved bending rods, to find out how effective adults with learning disabilities were at reorganizing information that is presented verbally or perceptually. (See Stone, 1987.) Stone concluded that some adults with learning disabilities are able to think abstractly and that the reasoning and problem-solving behaviors highlighted by the rods assessment process, are related to those that exist in certain academic and everyday problem situations, such as evaluating another person's assertion or conclusion (Stone, 1987, 77–78). The purpose of the task in Step Eight is to find out if learners are able to think in this way.

In fact, being able to complete Step Eight is critical for those learners in post-secondary or occupational situations requiring the ability to evaluate what they read and/or present a position or hypothesis in a research paper.

Results Indicating Problems in Abstract Reasoning

- inability to do the task at all;
- visible agitation;
- great difficulty thinking about the implications of the reading or summary;
- tendency to answer using what is already known and recorded rather than suggesting other possibilities;
- inability to draw any conclusions based on information given;
- lack of understanding of cause and effect relationships;
- ability to think abstractly only after probing questions are asked, examples given, and help offered in expanding answers;
- difficulty expressing verbally any thoughts or conclusions.

Examples of Results

Most learning disabled students find it very difficult to summarize and make decisions about what they have read, let alone analyze and evaluate possible conclusions and implications of what they have heard or written. Since thinking and reasoning abstractly requires an advanced stage of intellectual development, those educators conducting the HELP assessment may find that learning disabled participants cannot do Step Eight. If this is the case, they should simply make note of any difficulties and include compensatory strategies in learners' programs, such as signaling, graphic organizers, and adjunct-questioning techniques (see also Chapters 5 and 6).

Possible Formal Tests

Few formal tests measure abstract reasoning ability. However, two subtests of the DTLA-2 are helpful, as indicated on Figure 2-3.

- The Detroit Tests of Learning Aptitude (DTLA-2), Subtest V, "Story Construction" and Subtest VIII, "Symbolic Relations"

Where to Find Strategies
- Chapters 5 and 6
- Figures 3-2, 5-1, 6-1, 6-2 (examples)

Summary

The HELP assessment model cannot formally identify learning disabilities, nor can it uncover every learning problem. But, it *can* help adult educators make the following informal decisions:

- whether formal assessment is necessary;
- what kinds of learning difficulties can be expected; and
- which of the strategies outlined in this book will help to compensate for those learning problems.

The results of HELP can also be used as a yardstick against which to check formal assessment results.

HELP requires very little time and very few materials to administer. All learners need are paper and pencil, chart paper, highlighter pen, magic markers (optional), and a tape recorder and earphones. Educators need only paper or a booklet on which to record observations and reflections during the testing process, and an intuitive mind to make connections between observations and programming possibilities. By itself HELP takes about an hour and a half to complete. Should HELP be combined with the recommended formal tests, the total time required for both informal and formal testing is approximately three hours. Refer to Figure 2-3 for estimated times for each step.[1]

Now to the Compensatory Strategies

Chapter 3 is an overview of one category of compensatory supports and strategies—environmental supports and study skills—which are essential for people with learning disabilities who are about to embark on a journey into unknown territory.

---

[1] I invite the reader to try HELP, to test its validity, and to be part of the ongoing research process by contacting me through the publisher's address.

3

Environmental Supports and Study Strategies

Environmental supports and study strategies are designed to help compensate for learning-related deficits and to enable learning disabled adults to function in their everyday occupational and academic environments. These accommodations and aids may involve the use of special needs services, technical equipment, and management methods for studying.

This chapter is divided into three parts: (1) general supports (services and/or technical equipment provided by special needs counselors, faculty advocates, or human resource personnel); (2) study supports (organizational strategies to be used independently by learning disabled adults); and (3) instructional supports (multisensory and/or multidimensional teaching methods to be used by adult educators). (See Figure 3–1.)

(1) General Supports include:

- Orientation tours of the physical environment;
- Library tours in higher educational institutions;
- Reserved study carrels, office or locker space;
- Audiovisual devices;
- Technical supports, such as hearing and speech amplifiers and computers;
- Academic/staff advisors and advocates;
- Notetakers;
- Tutors and peer supports;
- Editorial and typing services.

(2) Study Supports include:

- A library research guide;
- Techniques for studying and taking tests;
- Color coding of materials.

(3) Instructional Supports include:

- Special arrangements, i.e. special seating, alternatives for taking tests or examinations, options for educational or work assignments;
- The use of audiovisual equipment and aids for teaching.

General Supports

Orientation of the Environment

Blalock and Johnson (1987, 43–44) state that all learning disabilities interfere, to a certain extent, with independence and daily functioning. Some learning disabled adult students say that they are constantly aware of their disabilities, which always seem to be part of them. Deficits in two particular areas, oral language and visual-spatial perception (remembering and processing information visually), can cause daily problems at school or in the work force. For example, inadequate oral language skills interfere with the ability to follow directions, recall information, and communicate with others. Visual-spatial disorders affect such simple activities as recognizing familiar neighborhood landmarks and finding the way around educational or occupational environments.

Therefore, orientation tours of where they will study or work are absolutely essential for people with learning disabilities. These tours should be part of the registration or start-up process, preferably a few weeks prior to starting classes or a new job.

Most educational institutions offer tours of the campus to anyone who wants to participate. However, general orientation tours tend to include all students, regardless of special learning needs, and are, more often than not, very noisy and confusing. It is unlikely that severely learning disabled individuals absorb and remember anything during such tours. Moreover, such

Figure 3-1: Overview of Environmental Supports

LEARNING PROBLEMS	INDIVIDUALIZED STRATEGIES & SUPPORTS FOR LEARNERS	CLASSROOM METHODS FOR INSTRUCTORS & TRAINERS
• has problems finding way around an environment	• orientation tours • faculty or staff advisor	
• finds it difficult to make decisions or solve problems	• faculty or staff advisor • faculty or staff advocate	• special arrangements for assignments and examinations
• has difficulties following or remembering verbal directions or processing auditory information	• tape recorder to record notes • notetaker • tutors and peer supports • hand-held laptop computers	• visual equipment (overhead) • visual screens
• course or job materials are disorganized	• colour-coded binders and file folders • reserved study carrel • office space or locker	
• has difficulties summarizing ideas in writing	• notetaker • tape recorder to record notes • tutors and peer supports • graphic or descriptive organizers	• visual equipment (overhead) • visual screens
• writes slowly or illegibly	• tape recorder to record notes • typing and editorial services	• special arrangements for assignments and examinations • use of visual equipment to provide extra time
• voice cannot be heard	• voice amplifier • peer tutor to speak on learner's behalf	• special seating arrangements
• is distractible in large groups or finds it difficult to concentrate	• tape recorder to record notes • earphones	• special arrangements • special examination arrangements • audiovisual equipment
• responds poorly to pressure	• orientation tours • faculty and staff advisor • faculty and staff advocate • test-taking SCORER strategy • tape recorder to record notes • tutors or peer supports • editorial and typing services	• special seating arrangements for assignments and examinations • special seating arrangements for classes

people are usually too unsure and embarrassed to ask questions or express concerns.

Either a second, or an individualized, tour should be made available for students with disabilities. This tour could include one or two participants and be conducted at an unhurried pace with many opportunities for questions and explanations to clear up confusion. There are several simple ways to arrange such tours, e.g. place a sign-up sheet in the special needs office or counseling department. However, an approach based on voluntary participation is not always adequate, and special efforts and arrangements may be necessary to reach special students.

Students with learning difficulties often: (1) don't know they need more assistance; (2) don't want to let any of their friends or acquaintances know they have special needs; (3) don't hear about the second tour; or (4) don't know where to find the sign-up list for the second orientation tour.

One effective method of reaching people who need a special tour is through registration packages (see Crux and O'Neill, 1988). A compulsory orientation tour of the educational setting could be a requirement for everyone with expressed concerns.

If an orientation tour is already compulsory for all students, the tour guides could provide details about a special, follow-up tour. In addition, all teachers could announce the availability of such a tour during the first few classes (for students who don't make it to the first class), explaining the purpose for the tours and where to sign up.

Orientation tours are as needed in occupational contexts as in educational settings—some industrial complexes are even larger than university or college campuses. Human resource trainers can arrange for orientation tours as described above. People who need help in finding their way around will also know someone to contact if they need additional or ongoing help.

However implemented and conducted, orientation tours will help meet the needs of learning disabled individuals who have difficulty finding their way around their environment.

Library Tours in Higher Education

In higher education settings, students simply cannot succeed without knowing how to do research for papers and assignments, and study for examinations; familiarity with the library and its procedures and resources is essential. Library tours are particularly important for those students with learning disabilities. They often have a hard time understanding instructions and following directions and may need extra help in order to be able to utilize the resources of a library.

Most educational settings offer tours of the library's facilities; in many universities a library tour is compulsory for every new student. And students often may elect to take additional tours by making a reservation with the reference librarian. Some institutions have a special needs librarian who will take students on an individualized tour, or will help them with particular assignments and study-related matters.

The library tour, even when individualized, is just a first step as learning disabled people often need further ongoing help. Certainly, knowing where to find materials in the library is a prerequisite for the compensatory strategies that follow.

Reserved Study Carrels or Office Space

People with learning problems are often personally and academically disorganized. They have trouble remembering or making decisions about what textbooks, course, or occupationally-related materials to bring to class or work. "I forgot" or "I didn't know we were supposed to bring that today" are familiar comments to all adult educators. A "reserved" study carrel or some personal work or office space can greatly reduce and compensate for problems of disorganization and forgetfulness. Learners can keep most of their materials at this special reserved location.

Arrangements to reserve a study carrel in an educational setting can be made by a special needs coordinator, someone in a faculty advocate role, a special needs librarian, a counseling staff member, or personnel in the registrar's office. Whoever provides this environmental support depends, to a great extent, on the administrative and special needs hierarchy at each institution.

Office space or shared space can usually be provided by human resource counselors, department heads, or sectional managers. If such space is not available, a private locker will suffice. Learning disabled people simply need somewhere to keep track of their retraining or work materials, such as basic reading books or a company manual.

Audiovisual Devices For Learners

There are several audio and visual aids that can be used to compensate for weakness in one or more areas of processing information through the auditory or visual senses. However, it is important that learners know which mode of learning works best for them. For example, it is not recommended that all students with learning problems be given the same type of auditory aid, such as taped textbooks or talking books (some learners perform better with visual aids) without some formal or informal assessment on which to base that decision. Too often, the first suggestions given to learning disabled persons when they return to school or undertake further training at work are the purchase or loan of a tape recorder and the ordering of taped textbooks.

In the section that follows two categories of audiovisual aids will be discussed: (1) taped textbooks, tape recorders, and earphones, and (2) visual screens.

Taped Textbooks, Tape Recorders, and Earphones

The most commonly used auditory aids are taped textbooks, tape recorders, and earphones. In a post-secondary setting, access to taped textbooks is usually arranged through a special needs counselor or reference librarian, in conjunction with the National Institute for the Blind and the Learning Disabilities Association. In occupational training situations, a human resource coordinator can arrange for such services, or they can be purchased privately. These aids need to be ordered at least six weeks in advance of their expected use.

Tape recorders have a multitude of uses. They allow students to listen to and take notes from taped textbooks. They can also be used to tape-record lectures or small group conversations for later transcription, which should always follow taping. A tape recorder should never be used as a substitute for notetaking; it is simply a compensatory device that allows for unhurried listening and writing—for later retrieval of information, taking of short-form notes, and organization of those notes (Vogel, 1987).

A mini-sized tape recorder can also be an effective memory aid, used in much the same way as a notepad, for learners who cannot remember instructions and have difficulty writing themselves reminder notes. People either listen to their own recorded messages (with earphones), as they would read a grocery list, or they record what they need to remember, and then transcribe that message later when they have both more time and privacy.

A tape recorder can sometimes be borrowed, but most learners should purchase one for themselves. A miniature-sized recorder, with a small tape called a microcassette, is easy to manipulate or carry in a purse or gym bag. Also recommended is the purchase or loan of a pair of earphones. Although taped textbooks or other taped materials can be heard without earphones, comprehension of material, when either listening or notetaking, seems to be greatly increased with their use. Distractions are reduced and listening skills are strengthened.

The use of earphones and tape recorders will be recommended throughout this book because they are invaluable when reading for comprehension, listening and notetaking, and organizing and writing notes and assignments.

Visual Screens

Visual screens, usually required for visually impaired people, are also valuable aids for individuals with learning disabilities. These supports must be purchased by educational and other institutions, and are usually reserved by special needs counselors or the instructors and trainers in whose class the participants are registered. Visual screens include: (1) chalkboards; (2) chart pads; (3) opaque or transparent surfaces for films, filmstrips, or slides; or (4) video or computer monitors.

Visual screens are used to keep track of important points discussed during lectures and classes. They can also be very helpful for the hearing impaired learning disabled in combination with the services of a dicta-typist (discussed in the next section). A visual presentation of material is extremely helpful for people who find it difficult to process and remember instructions and information through their auditory sense alone.

Technical Assisting Devices and Technical Support Personnel

Technical assisting devices can range from auditory amplifiers, to the equipment used by dicta-typists for learning disabled people who have a hearing impairment, to microcomputers and word processing aids with spelling and thesaurus features. Voice amplifiers are also available for learners who have trouble speaking loudly enough to be heard in a classroom or work situation. Both auditory and voice amplifiers are technical, specialized devices and need to be purchased privately by learners or borrowed from a counseling or special needs office.

A dicta-typist is a volunteer or staff member assigned to assist individuals with learning problems in writing and hearing. If participants are unable to write quickly enough when notetaking is required, or if they have a hearing impairment in addition to their learning disabilities, the criteria for providing a dicta-typist have been met.

Computers can provide effective support if learners have acquired the prerequisite skills to use them. Since not all learning disabled people can type successfully, training in typing and how to use the hardware should be offered. Assuming learners are ready to use this type of equipment, who can benefit and when?

For learners who are visually oriented, and especially for those individuals with listening and writing problems, computers are excellent tools to reinforce what is being learned. For example, learners can use the computer to make summary notes of their tape recorded classroom notes. (More will be said about computer usage in the Chapters 5 and 6 on reading comprehension and notetaking strategies.)

Also on the market today are computer-based organizers with exchange-able cards (e.g. the Sharp IQ-7000, with a calendar and dictionary/thesaurus cards) and hand-held laptop computers for on-the-spot notetaking. This hardware can be linked to an IBM compatible personal computer for data transfer and copy printing. Learners would have to be taught how to use this technical equipment. As a point of interest, some palm-sized laptop comput-ers have alphabetized keyboards instead of the usual layout. This can help a non-typist, but can be extremely frustrating for people with even marginal typing skills. (For a complete review of this type of equipment, refer to Stevenson, 1991.)

Academic/Staff Advising and Advocacy

Advisor

People with learning difficulties also need someone to help them plan their program and arrange for support services. This person may be an instructor or trainer, or someone in the workplace, such as a special needs coordinator or human resource counselor. Whoever does the advising and counseling must help learners consider and make decisions about course selection, number of courses, balance of courses, timetabling, or the most appropriate retraining format.

Course selections must be made on the basis of complete, accurate infor-mation, including whether or not learners have the necessary background, skills, or prerequisites, and/or if the subjects are appropriate to learners' interests and abilities.

Timetabling is extremely important—the way courses are scheduled can mean the difference between success and failure. For example, for people with long-term memory deficits, the more frequently the instructor evaluates students, the better. In addition, these students benefit from classes that meet three or four times a week as opposed to those that meet for an extended class period only once a week (Vogel, 1987, 251).

The course load must also be manageable. A regular schedule of fifteen to eighteen credit hours per week at the university level, or twenty-four hours at the community college level, is just not reasonable when many new compensatory strategies must also be acquired. Blalock (1981) suggests that a reduced credit load is a must if learners are to successfully complete what they start (e.g. nine to fourteen hours, respectively). In fact, Vogel (1987, 251) says that some students may achieve better results if enroled on a part-time basis, especially at the beginning of their college careers when they are trying to acquire so many new and complex skills. However, the part-time option is not always possible given the criteria for some scholarships and student loan programs.

In occupational retraining, upgrading, professional development, or literacy classes, responsibilities must also be arranged to avoid overloading learners. If, for example, they are working a full shift before attending classes, something will suffer, and it may be the job. If at all possible, try to schedule retraining or professional development during the regular working day or shift.

Advocate

The responsibilities of the advocate are somewhat different, although the same person may both advise and act as an advocate. The major role of an advocate is to educate faculty or management that the "invisible" learning needs of learning disabled students or personnel are genuine. Faculty or human resource staff need to know what kind of problems students have and what they can do to help. Vogel (1987, 252) states that the majority of faculty members and administrators welcome the opportunity to acquire this new information and become more sensitive to learners' unique patterns of strengths and weaknesses, their difficulties, and their determination to persevere.

With the provision of advisor and advocacy services comes the danger of dependence. However, the clearly articulated goal is that over time participants themselves will acquire self-advocacy skills and no longer have to rely on such support. This is in keeping with the aim common to all compensatory strategies—that learners will gradually move towards self-direction. But, until learners are ready for such independence, ongoing assistance and intervention are needed.

Notetakers

Notetakers are offered by some educational institutions or in industry for people who cannot take notes. This service is usually reserved for people who have multiple disabilities, such as learning and physical disabilities and a hearing impairment. However, if cost or availability of staff or volunteers to act as notetakers is not at issue, these services could be made available to those individuals with learning disabilities that affect the writing act itself (e.g. severe problems with speed or accuracy).

In college or university settings, notetakers are usually seated beside or behind the learners they are helping. As this service is also intended to free students to get more out of class lectures or seminar discussions, they are expected primarily to listen to the instructor, and *only* look at what the notetaker is writing if there is a lull in the discussion. If learners require assistance with notetaking, they must spend the time that they would have struggled with writing listening to the material being presented. Trying to listen and watch the notetaker at the same time is less productive than receiving no support assistance at all.

In very special circumstances, notetakers will actually go to an educational setting in place of students, e.g. when learning disabled people in wheelchairs have classes in rooms without access.

Notetakers can also be used effectively in business and industry for people who must attend union or board meetings, but are unable to take notes. In this situation the notes can be taken by someone who is also attending the meeting so that the person with learning problems will not be singled out. Carbonless multiple copy formats are now available for this purpose.

Whatever the setting, notetaking services are very helpful for those learning disabled individuals who have handwriting problems or multiple disabilities and who could not otherwise take or transcribe notes.

Tutors and Peer Supports

Tutors and peer support services are available in some community college, university, and occupational training situations. Peers, who have received specialized training, are used to assist learning disabled people with notetaking (outside of class) and editorial tasks. Tutors may teach participants necessary compensatory strategies, taking the place of instructors and trainers. They may offer guidance to students who need to learn where to get and how to use the various supports discussed in this chapter, such as individualized tours of the physical buildings or the library. They may review library skills and supervise study sessions or teach learners how to type in order to use a computer.

Essentially, peer-tutors are involved in a co-learning relationship for the purpose of helping learning disabled adults move from a dependent learner role to a more self-directed position.

Editorial and Typing Services

It is very important to make available editorial and typing services for adults with learning problems. In higher education such services can be provided by volunteers or peer supports, or by students working on an hourly basis. In industry, clerical or secretarial personnel can offer these services.

It is clearly *not* the responsibility of editors to rewrite the work of students or employees. It must be made very clear, before the editing is done, that the editor will not make revisions and corrections; learners must understand that the writing is to be theirs. However, editors can point out glaring errors in style, grammar, spelling, and punctuation. They can also recommend that work should be done again.

Once the editing process is complete and learners have corrected the work to the best of their ability, it should be typed. However, learning disabled people often either do not type, or type too slowly to meet deadlines. Therefore, typing services may also be necessary for learning disabled individuals with illegible or erratic handwriting. (Later chapters will discuss techniques to compensate for poor handwriting, e.g. graphic organizers, word processing programs with spellcheck features.)

In addition to keying in material, typing services can provide an additional benefit for people with learning problems by acting as a final editing service, checking for spelling and grammatical errors that were missed. It is ideal when typing and editing services are available on a continuous basis to provide assistance no matter how many times work has to be checked or typed.

Study Supports

Study supports are intended primarily for learning disabled people in educational settings and include library and test-taking strategies and course management methods. However, simple modifications in the techniques can be made by industrial trainers in literacy and retraining programs to meet their needs. For example, if company personnel need to acquire certain information as part of their employment (e.g. a clear understanding of safety standards or routines), the library study skills format discussed next can be adapted.

Library Study Skills

Many skills are required to be able to research and find materials in a library. (Reading, notetaking, summarizing, and writing will be covered in other chapters.) Presented here is a method designed to enable adults with learning disabilities to organize and structure their preliminary library time to research an assignment, such as an essay, class presentation, or test. Please refer to Figure 3–2, the library research worksheet.

In most cases, this research method is taught and supervised by a special needs counselor or a volunteer tutor. It is especially helpful if the general topic for research is provided by the instructor, who will then be kept informed of any difficulties and progress. This worksheet contains six steps.

- *Step One:* Students decide what they are looking for. They choose a topic or, at the least, begin to narrow down an area of interest to a possible topic. To aid this process they should pose the familiar

Who, What, When, Where, and *Why* questions twice: once to reduce or more clearly define the topic, and once to establish the limits of argument or discussion. In the first instance, therefore, these questions assist in concept and topic clarification and in the second, using this approach will help students clarify what they need to discover from their research and what must be presented in their paper. Once they have made a selection, they write a brief summary of what their topic is about on the worksheet in the section labelled Step One.

- *Step Two:* The next step is to consult the manual card catalogue or on-line computer terminal in the library to find material on that topic (e.g. books or journal titles). If students do not know how to use the manual or computerized catalogue, that skill should be taught first. Appropriate sources are recorded in the Step Two section of the worksheet. Also in this section, students should note subject topics and headings that might be useful in further checks through the library catalogue.
- Step Three: Record the call numbers from the card in the catalogue. Encourage students to include call numbers of any material that might contain information related to their topics or initial ideas. Students then locate these books or journals, and quickly skim through each at the shelves to see if they have useful information.
- Step Four: Once students decide to keep a book or journal, either to sign out or to read in the library or their study carrel, they check off the box beside that call number to keep track of their selections.
- *Step Five:* Learners write citations. They should be taught how to do this correctly, using the style manual appropriate for their subject specialization. (In the example in Figure 3–2, the APA format is used, from the *Publication Manual of the American Psychological Association.*) This step is essential because learning disabled adult students often lose and can't locate sources when writing papers or drawing up the bibliography. In addition, this task gives learners practice in writing proper citations.
- *Step Six:* The final step of this worksheet consists of writing a brief summary and any quotations that might be needed for later use in an assignment or examination.

This library skills compensatory strategy, in combination with other research and reading strategies, can teach learners the following basic library research skills:

- how to clarify the purpose of research by defining the topic;
- how to find what is available in the card catalogue;
- how to judge which sources should be used and which discarded;
- how to write citations;
- how to decide what to include in notes and quotations.

Figure 3-2: Library Research Worksheet

Step One: Topic/Ideas in Brief	Step Two: Catalogue Subject Headings
Example: Personal Change and Retirement	*Example:* Adult Learning Journals for 1989 and 1990

Step Three: Identify Call Numbers
Step Four: Check Call Numbers to Be Used (✓)

Example: LC 5201/A33 Nov 1989 Vol. 1.3	☑		☐
	☐		☐
	☐		☐
	☐		☐

Step Five: Copy Complete Citations of References Chosen	Step Six: Notes, Quotes, and Page Numbers for Each Reference
(1)*Example:* Knowles, M.S. (1989), Learning after retirement. <u>Adult Learning</u> 1(3), 8-10.	(1)*Example:* This article outlines various activities Knowles engages in since retirement(e.g. reading, writing, attending conferences, conducting workshops, traveling). A good example of how productive people undergoing late-life change can be. Quote: "Survivors tended to be strongly future-oriented, while non-survivors tended to be past-oriented." (pp. 9)
(2)	(2)
(3)	(3)
(4)	(4)
(5)	(5)

However, never assume students have acquired any of these skills: it may be necessary to teach each of the library study skill steps individually before the whole process can be undertaken.

Test-taking

SCORER:

SCORER is a memory (mnemonic) device to be used when writing an examination or test. Learners are expected to memorize what each individual letter represents and then consciously use this knowledge to guide what they do and when they do it. They should write the letters at the top of their examination page and then check off each step as it is completed. The purpose of this device is to teach students how to *answer the question.* Getting to the root of the question is particularly important for test success.

In brief, SCORER means:

S - schedule your time;
C - find clues in the examination questions;
O - omit the difficult questions;
R - read the questions carefully;
E - estimate time needed to complete the examination;
R - review your work.

SCORER is intended to remind students of three basic tasks to be completed when writing examinations: (1) scheduling and estimating time—S, E, and the final R; (2) reading the questions and deciding which questions to answer—the first R and O; and (3) finding clues in the questions chosen to make sure they are answered appropriately—C (Towle, 1982). The strategy usually is carried out simultaneously rather than sequentially. For example, students will decide which questions to omit as they are reading them carefully for clues.

Learning disabled people with memory and organizational deficits find it extremely difficult to plan how to write an examination, especially when more than one question is included. SCORER reminds learners that their first step must be to check how many questions are on the test and how much time is available to answer them. The S stands for "scheduling" appropriate time. The E refers to "estimating" the appropriate length of time to devote to each question, and the final R to saving time for "reviewing" what was written.

The second R is a reminder to "read" the questions very carefully, the O prompts learners to "omit" the most difficult questions, assuming there is choice, and the C refers to finding the key or "clue" words or phrases in the examination questions that define what must be included in an answer. Students need to be aware of and look for terms like: discuss, explain, compare and contrast, analyze, and express an opinion. They must be able to find and identify these kinds of words and phrases so that they will be sure to answer the questions appropriately.

Self-questioning

Self-questioning is one of the most widely used ways of preparing for tests and examinations. Learners simply make up a few questions that might be asked and then answer them in detail. In the case of learning disabled participants, it may be necessary for the instructor or a special needs counselor to provide some sample test questions.

Students try to answer the questions as they would in a real test. Two aspects of this technique make it such a valuable strategy. First, individuals learn the content or skills required (e.g. in a carpentry or machinist course) by having to prepare and complete the trial questions. Second, learners get experience in writing examination answers, whether in essay or other form.

Self-questioning could be effective in industrial settings as well. For example, employees are frequently required to answer questions about their jobs or other duties. The self-questioning technique could be used by workers to prepare for when they must demonstrate that they have the required knowledge and skills. The employees would, of course, have to practice using the strategy beforehand. This instructional responsibility is usually assumed by a human resource coordinator.

Course Management

Many people, with or without learning disabilities, have serious problems with personal, job, or academic management strategies. It is not uncommon to find desks littered with all kinds of materials with no recognizable organization. Some of us somehow manage in spite of the chaos. For the most part, for learning disabled people this disorganization is the norm and affects not only the way their desks and homes look but also whatever they do or try to do in their lives. A very simple technique can compensate for this problem: the use of color-coded binders and file folders. (Color coding will also appear in the next chapter on time management strategies.)

Color Coding Educational/Work Materials

Learners purchase or acquire a differently colored binder for every course they take or for every job they have. They should also obtain a few colored file folders that co-ordinate with these binders. This simple and straightforward strategy is extremely effective. If they also have a reserved study carrel, office space, or locker, learners can keep the color-coded materials close at hand, instantly recognizable by color.

For example, college students taking three courses would obtain three binders, blue, red, and green. The corresponding file folders would also be blue, red, and green respectively, and course handouts or returned assignments that had no other place to go would be stored in the folder associated with the course.

This use of color coding can also be helpful to people in job training situations. Using again the example of safety standards and regulations education, employees could have a different binder for each of the various problems. A green binder could contain material on standard safety procedures, a yellow binder could include instructions in handling hazardous wastes, and a red one could have emergency routines. Other arrangements can be made for those who are color-blind, e.g. binder covers with different designs, such as black lines on a white background.

Instructional Supports

Special Arrangements

There are at least three special arrangements that can be made on behalf of learning disabled students or for which they can ask. Requests may be made by an assigned faculty advocate or students themselves. Some counseling centres offer assertiveness training courses to help students make special requests. The most widely used special arrangements are: (1) seating, (2) examinations, and (3) assignments.

Seating

Seating can present real problems for learning disabled students who have auditory discrimination or vocal problems, especially in large lecture halls. They simply cannot hear what is being said, either by the instructor or other students. Nor do they dare try to speak and be heard themselves. In such circumstances, arrangements should by made for these learning disabled participants to sit as close to the front and centre as is possible.

The desks provided in classrooms for taking notes can also present problems—some desk tops are so small that it is difficult to write. Average students somehow manage, but these circumstances add to the overall frustration of people with learning problems. Special arrangements can be made for a different seat and writing surface.

Examinations

Writing an examination in a hall with several hundred people is difficult for anyone, but is particularly distracting and stressful for people who cannot concentrate easily. The time limits of examinations add further pressure for those who have trouble writing and thinking quickly. As a result, learning disabled individuals simply cannot function at their peak performance level. Considering the time and effort required for learning disabled students to complete essay assignments while using compensatory techniques, writing a successful paper in a short period of time is very difficult—in some instances, impossible.

There are other ways of taking examinations, and special arrangements can be made to use them. For example, four alternatives are: (1) oral examinations; (2) take-home examinations; (3) completing the examination at the same time as everyone else, but in a room alone; and (4) completing the examination in the same room and within the same time period as everyone else, but with the option of more time if it is necessary.

Students should be allowed whatever method of test-taking is best for them, given their learning strengths and weaknesses. Most post-secondary institutions will allow for such options as long as academic standards are not lowered. (Bursuck, Rose, Cowen & Yahaya, 1989).

Assignments

Assignments are the area over which instructors have the most latitude to make special arrangements. Essays and formal examinations are not the only ways to measure learning. If students have severe problems organizing and writing, other assignments can be given that require a similar level of research, but capitalize on other skills. Some suggestions are:

- interviews and reports;
- ongoing response journals;
- class presentations alone or with someone else;
- case study reports;
- mini-research projects in a community setting;
- annotated bibliographies; or
- summaries of films, records or books.

There are many books on instructional techniques that will provide other ideas (cf. Cranton, 1989).

Another special arrangement is to grant an extension, beyond the due date, for the completion of an assignment. If learners are working closely with a special needs counselor on compensatory strategies that include goal setting and timetabling, extensions may not be necessary. However, if not, adult educators can help disorganized students by extending the required completion date, remembering that disorganization is a manifestation of most learning disabilities.

Audiovisual Instructional Equipment

Multisensory equipment can be used by instructors on a day-to-day basis, not just for special needs students. A standard lecture format reaches only those individuals who are good listeners and notetakers and may not provide effective instruction for half or more of the class. In order to reach all students (and not just those with learning disabilities), a variety of both audio and visual methods must be used.

Some of the more widely used audio techniques include video-cassette film recordings and 16mm movies. Closed caption techniques, which include both sound and written speech, were developed for the hearing impaired, but they are extremely helpful for learning disabled students who can see the pictures and the written words, as well as hear the words being spoken. Other visual aids include overhead projectors, filmstrip projectors, slide projectors, laminated posters and pictures, charts, maps, and diagrams.

All visual aids should relate directly to what is being taught at the moment. For example, a nursing instructor who is teaching how to give an injection can lecture on the topic while pointing to a chart and/or diagram of precautions and routines. At the same time, an overhead projector transparency, listing what is being said to the class, can be shown. And finally, the technique can then be demonstrated to students. The use of a variety of audiovisual aids stimulates both visual and auditory senses, helping learners grasp skills and content more effectively than from lecturing alone.

Summary

This chapter has presented an overview of various environmental aids and accommodations, also known as compensatory supports and study strategies. Methods have been outlined that will help both learners and adult educators. The next chapter discusses goal setting and time management strategies and techniques that help learning disabled people organize their time and their responsibilities. These skills are absolutely essential for the completion of educational programs or success in employment.

4

Goal Setting and Time Management

All of us, from time to time, become disorganized. But we know better and have the ability to do something about it when we need to. However, learning disabled people seldom realize their full potential often because of poor planning habits and an inability to prioritize activities and complete assignments (Johnson & Blalock, 1987b, 280). And in addition, because they also have inadequate self-monitoring skills, learning disabled individuals do not even realize that they are not effective organizers.

The purpose of this chapter is to outline a variety of goal setting and time and course management strategies that, when used on a regular basis, can help people with learning problems compensate for their lack of organizational skills. Some of these methods must be taught in individualized programs by special needs counselors or human resource trainers. Others can be used by instructors or trainers in large group, classroom situations. The methods can be used in either educational or industrial settings. The materials or aids needed to teach these compensatory strategies are: course outlines, calendars, index cards, colored markers and pencils, tape recorders and earphones, computerized organizers with a calendar feature, and microcomputers and word processing programs. Refer to Figure 4–1 for an overview of the strategies, aids, and instructional applications.

The first section of this chapter outlines the following *Instructional Management* approaches to be implemented by instructors and trainers:

- the use of course outlines to help learners organize themselves through proper planning and goal setting; and

- the use of classroom techniques that provide an organizational framework for timetabling and time management.

(Although the term "course outlines" suggests an educational setting, they can be used in any adult education context.)

In the second section, *Learner Self-management*, five areas of interest to learners in a semester or year-long program and their counselors will be discussed. This is not to suggest that the same techniques cannot be useful in short-term occupational training situations. They can, and examples will be provided where feasible. The points of discussion are the following:

- seasonal/monthly goal setting;
- weekly goal setting;
- daily timetabling and goal setting;
- time-of-day management; and
- length-of-study management.

Instructional Management

Using Course Outlines

Course outlines range in length and complexity from one-page overviews to in-depth notes. All students, but particularly those with learning disabilities, need detailed outlines to clarify what is expected of them throughout the term, in order to set short- and long-term academic goals and develop a personalized academic calendar. Unfortunately, too many outlines do not indicate what materials have to be read, when assignments are due, and when tests and examinations are scheduled.

To help individuals with learning disabilities, course outlines should include the topic of each lecture or series of lectures, the reading(s) for those lectures, and specific reminders and dates for assignments and examinations. An example of this format is as follows:

Week of:　　　　October 8th

Topic:　　　　　Using Learning Contracts in Teacher Education

Figure 4-1: Overview of Goal Setting and Time Management Strategies

LEARNING PROBLEMS	INDIVIDUALIZED STRATEGIES & SUPPORTS FOR LEARNERS	CLASSROOM METHODS FOR INSTRUCTORS & TRAINERS
• has difficulty making decisions	• index cards • color coding • calendars	• course outlines • class instructions (verbal and visual)
• tends to be disorganized and forgetful	• calendars • microcomputer software • calendar program organizer • graphic organizers and lists	• class instructions (verbal and visual) • course outlines
• does not know how to organize time	• index cards • electronic organizers (e.g. Sharp IQ-7000 Time Manager Card) • color coding • calendars (on paper)	
• has problems prioritizing duties	• index cards • color coding • sequencing charts	• course outlines • class instructions (verbal and visual)
• can't predict problems or consequences	• calendars • diary	
• has difficulty starting and completing tasks	• diary for time-of-day and length-of-time management	• course outlines with dates • class timetabling
• does not do assignments or hands them in late	• index cards • calendars	• course outlines with dates
• forgets classes or appointments	• calendars • computerized calculator//calendar • tape recorder and earphones	• course outlines • class timetabling and instructions
• loses goal-setting materials	• computerized calculator/calendar • tape recorder & earphones • microcomputer software calendar program	• course outlines with semester structure

Readings: (1) Knowles, M.S. (1986). *Using Learning Contracts.* San Francisco, CA: Jossey-Bass.

(2) Caffarella, R.S., and E.P. Caffarella (1986). Self-directedness and learning contracts in adult education. *Adult Education Quarterly,* 36 (4), 226-234.

Reminders: (1) Critique of the film *Educating Rita.*

Although this course outline format is extensive, when used, it benefits all students, but especially those with learning disabilities. For instructors in hands-on courses (e.g. auto mechanics), the same format could be used, except the "readings" category might be replaced with the "skills" to be learned.

Course outlines can also be useful in occupational training situations. For example, a literacy training instructor can prepare a similar outline before a series of individual or small group meetings. If participants are not yet able to read, the instructor can make available a short audio cassette tape of what is going to occur. If they can read, but not well, a graphic organizer can be developed, using drawings or magazine pictures to represent and sequence the events and topics coming up in the days or weeks ahead.

Class Timetabling and Special Instructions

Regardless of how detailed course outlines may be, instructors and trainers are occasionally ahead or behind schedule. There are several useful instructional techniques to assist learning disabled people keep track of what occurs in each class they attend and what to expect for the next class.

The instructor writes a short agenda on the chalkboard or chart at the start of every class and briefly records objectives for that class in a point-form list. This simple technique prepares all students (with or without learning disabilities) for where the class is going and how the content/skills of that day relate to topics listed on the course outline.

Another practical suggestion is to end each class with a few verbal and written instructions on the chalkboard, or possibly on an overhead transparency, on the topics of the next class and how learners can prepare for it.

Detailed course outlines, written objectives at the start of every class, and a wrap-up of what to expect for the next session, enable learning disabled people to set goals and manage their time more effectively.

These techniques can be modified for use in industrial training settings. The same in-class agenda, explaining what the current class will be about, and final wrap-up, stating what needs to be done before the next session, are as useful here as in any other instructional situation. If participants find writing difficult, they can use a tape recorder for dictating instructions. When tape recorders are part of the training process, it is unlikely learners will be hesitant to use them. However, if they are reluctant to dictate in class, suggest doing this in the privacy of their office or car, before going home. If the topic lends itself to visual presentation (e.g. a safety poster), that format could itself act as a timetabling and training outline.

Learner Self-Management

Seasonal/Monthly Goal Setting

Assigning a Date for Completion

The process of seasonal/monthly goal setting requires students to find out the dates by which all assignments, readings, and examinations must be completed or written. Learners must use every source of information available, including course outlines and handouts. If this material does not contain enough information, participants can make appointments with each of their professors. With diary in hand, they must establish exact dates and requirements for all lectures, labs, seminars, tutorials, or practica.

Once the necessary information has been gathered, seasonal or monthly calendars must be obtained. Then, ask students to write a list (in pencil) of all tasks for a whole semester, (e.g. from September to December). When the list is completed, students reread and prioritize every item—what must be done first, second, and so on. This itemizing process may take from two to three hours to complete; it often requires several attempts to get the list properly sequenced.

Figure 4-2: Seasonal/Monthly List	
Example of a Prioritized Seasonal/Monthly List	
Course/Topic: Psychology 100	**Priority**
• 1000-word essay on child development due December 6th	4th
• act as seminar leader for class of October 16th	2nd
• midterm exam on November 29th	3rd
• visit to a child-oriented community organization on September 30th	1st

Once the list is completed and corrected, students who are working with counselors or tutors may transfer all their information on to a large laminated seasonal calendar to be kept in the instructor's office. Color-coded water soluble markers allow students to choose separate colors for each course.

Students then transfer the information to their smaller (e.g. usually slightly larger than 8½ by 11) monthly calendars. Again they may color-code, but this time using colored pencil crayons, to individualize the assignment and work-related requirements for each course. Finally, students should save their prioritized list in a file folder that carries an "assignment information" label, in case they lose their monthly calendars!

Long-term calendars can be used in employment and training situations in the same way. Personnel counselors and staff would identify what is to be done during the next few months and write these goals on a seasonal calendar. This information can be entered into large day planners for employees' desk tops.

Weekly Goal Setting

Breaking Down Assignments into Steps

After long-range goal setting and timetabling have been completed, shorter-term goals must be identified. This process involves dividing assignments or jobs into smaller tasks and deciding in what order each should be done (Stone, 1981), and is especially hard for people with learning disabilities. In order to complete a job, learn a new skill, or finish an academic assignment, they must be able to structure their lives and activities around

Figure 4-3: Seasonal Organizer

Example of Seasonal/Monthly Goal Setting for Time Management

SEPTEMBER							NOVEMBER						
Sun	Mon	Tues	Wed	Thur	Fri	Sat	Sun	Mon	Tues	Wed	Thur	Fri	Sat
1	2	3	4	5	6	7						1	2
8	9	10	11	12	13	14	3	4	5	6	7	8	9
15	16	17	18	19	20	21	10	11	12	13	14	15	16
22	23	24	25	26	27	28	17	18	19	20	21	22	23
29	30 Psych 100 community visit						24	25	26	27	28	29 Psych 100 exam	30

OCTOBER							DECEMBER						
Sun	Mon	Tues	Wed	Thur	Fri	Sat	Sun	Mon	Tues	Wed	Thur	Fri	Sat
		1	2	3	4	5	1	2	3	4	5	6 Psych 100 essay	7
6	7	8	9	10	11	12	8	9	10	11	12	13	14
13	14	15	16 Psych 100 seminar	17	18	19	15	16	17	18	19	20	21
20	21	22	23	24	25	26	22	23	24	25	26	27	28
27	28	29	30	31			29	30	31				

getting that work done, on time, and to the best of their abilities. Weekly timetabling is a strategy that helps employees and students with learning problems meet their responsibilities on schedule.

To begin the process, participants review their long range calendar. They label at least ten 5 × 8 index cards for each course or job responsibility they have. For example, students taking Psychology 100 would label their ten cards *Psych 100* with the appropriate color-coded pencil crayon. They would do the same for all their courses.

When cards have been labelled, ideas on how to complete each step on the monthly calendar are recorded on the cards. If more than ten cards are needed, put labels on additional cards as required. Disregard any surplus. If teaching this strategy in a private tutorial or small group, "brainstorming" or generating ideas together can be helpful. No attempt should be made at this point to sequence ideas; the task is to suggest and record as many ideas as possible. For example, what is necessary for the preparation and completion of an essay for a psychology course? Entries might read as follows:

- locate Library of Congress subject headings;
- look up the sources;
- decide which sources are relevant;
- make rough notes;
- structure the notes into an organizer;
- write the introduction;
- write the body of the paper;
- write the summary and conclusions;
- revise the paper;
- proofread and make corrections;
- take to an editor;
- get final typing done;
- hand it in.

After individual work or group brainstorming on each course is complete and all ideas have been recorded (this process may take several hours or work sessions), students reread their index cards and prioritize tasks for each course—what is to be done first, second, and so on. This can be done with marker or colored pencils color-coded for the appropriate course (e.g. see previous chapter on course management). All cards associated with each course then should be stapled together. Thus, the processes of brainstorming and prioritizing enable learners to set goals and break down assignments into small, manageable, bite-sized chunks (Gagne, 1987).

Now learners are ready to transfer the items on their cards to their weekly calendars, which preferably have a "week-at-a-glance" feature. Students should continue to use the color codes for each course and related step, preferably numbering each step in that appropriate color as well. Computerized organizers with calendars can also be used for this process. People who have difficulty writing can tape-record the steps that need to be done to complete their assignments and, using earphones, can type this information into a computer. The ideas then do not have to be sequenced prior to data entry. Once they are on disk they can be rearranged in order.

Figure 4-4: Example of Prioritized Index Cards

Weekly Goal Setting for Time Management

Example of Two Index Cards for Psychology 100 Essay

Psychology 100 Essay
Due: December 6th
Planning: week of Nov. 10th

P.1 Using the sources already read and briefly summarized, develop a list of most important points

P.2 Make a graphic organizer showing how points interrelate

P.3 Summarize the organizer in sentences using the tape recorder

---

Psychology 100 Essay
Due: December 6th
Writing: week of Nov. 10th

W.1 Using earphones, type what was previously taped

W.2 Print out that information

W.3 Revise, adding any more pertinent information

W.4 Retape, adding an introduction and conclusion

W.5 Retype, print out, and check that body of paper and conclusions are consistent with introduction

W.6 Check references

Key:

P - Planning Process

W - Writing Process (First Draft)

Figure 4-5: Weekly Organizer

Week of November 10th

	Sunday 10	Monday 11	Tuesday 12	Wednesday 13	Thursday 14	Friday 15	Saturday 16
8:30-9:30		Psych 100 P.3					Psych 100 W.6
9:30-10:30	Psych 100 P.1						
10:30-11:30							
11:30-12:30							
12:30-1:30				Psych 100 W.1		Psych 100 W.3	
1:30-2:30	Psych 100 P.2						
2:30-3:30							
3:30-4:30							
4:30-7:00				Psych 100 W.2			
7:00-10:00						Psych 100 W.4 W.5	

Daily Timetabling

Assigning Individual Dates for Completion

Although it may seem unnecessary, given the amount of planning and organization already carried out, a further division of weekly goals into even smaller steps on a *daily* calendar is essential for learners with time and organizational difficulties. Most of us keep track of daily tasks automatically; learning disabled people do not. Now is the time to do it. Some of the larger tasks involve several steps, such as preparing rough notes and graphic organizers. Even simple tasks, such as locating subject headings and potential sources in the library, may take more time than anticipated. Short-term daily planning also involves noting personal and business responsibilities, e.g. dental appointments, grocery shopping, or management meetings.

Learners return to the original index cards and color-coding tasks completed earlier. If there is room on these cards, they write the substeps under each of the primary steps identified on the priority list. If there is not enough space, they use a different index card and rewrite each step in more detail. All additional index cards are stapled to each group of course cards, or the information may be entered on a computerized organizer/calendar. Once a day, learners or employees can check their calendar programs to make additions or deletions and take note of what has to be done that day. This type of technical program is especially helpful for people with handwriting difficulties.

The simplest way to keep track of daily tasks and events is to use a mnemonic device—a memory technique to aid recall. Based on the old construction signs that read "Men At Work," is "AT WORC," a mnemonic device students may find useful. In this case, the phrase refers to the fact that they are at work; the individual letters stand for:

> A—Appointments (school or otherwise),
> T—Time in the library,
>
> W—Writing (essays/notes),
> O—Other activities,
> R—Reading (course work/research sources),
> C—Classes.

Some students use these letters or "codes" when they are entering information on to their calendars using their colored pencils, again color-coded appropriately according to course. They are equally useful for the computerized calculator calendars because only one letter is required plus the course assignment.

Entries might look like this:

Friday, October 5th

    1 PM **A** (Dentist)
    2 PM **C** (Psych 100 Seminar) *written in red*
    3 PM
    4 PM **R** (Read for Psych 100: Kemp, pp.23–40) *written in red*
    5 PM
    6 PM **O** (David's birthday barbecue)

Whatever method works best for learners should be used to structure a daily schedule. In the above example, the title for the course is not really necessary as the *C* and *R* would be marked in the color (in this case, red) chosen for the particular course.

Daily timetabling is also useful for people at work. Employees traditionally have used in/out boxes, file systems, calendars, etc. to organize activities according to importance and/or schedule. Computer planning programs (e.g. To Do Lists) are also helpful, especially when more than one person must keep track of long- and short-term goals.

Summary of Goal Setting and Time Management Strategies

The following is a summary of each of the goal setting and time management steps.

Seasonal/Monthly

Learners should be able to:

- make a list of all the major assignments required during the semester, with their completion dates (e.g. when an essay is due, when an examination is scheduled);
- list tasks in order of importance (what must be done first, second, and so on);
- transfer the prioritized items to a seasonal or monthly calendar, color coding each course (or job responsibility).

Refer to Figures 4–2 and 4–3.

Figure 4-6: Daily Organizer Using AT WORC	
Friday, November 15	
8:30-9:30	**C** (8:30-10:30, Psychology 100, Room S107) **R** (Mayer, 1987, pp. 18-43, for Psych)
9:30-10:30	
10:30-11:30	**O** (Student Council Meeting)
11:30-12:30	
12:30-1:30	**W** (W.3)
1:30-2:30	
2:30-3:30	
3:30-4:30	**A** (Dentist)
4:30-7:00	**O** (Dinner Out-Marg)
7:00-10:00	**W** (W.4 & W.5)

A - Appointment

T - Time in library

W - Writing

O - Other activities

R - Reading

C - Classes

Note: Although only one course is shown in the example above (which would be color-coded), other entries would be shown as well and also identified by their course color.

Weekly

Learners should be able to:

- label ten (more or less as required) 5 × 8 index cards for *each* course or job;
- using those index cards, for *each* course, record every step that has to be done for each course assignment or job, using appropriately colored pencils (e.g. preliminary research in the library, developing a graphic organizer, writing a first draft, and so on);
- prioritize the information on these index cards, e.g. what has to be done first, second, and so on;
- then, transfer the information from the index cards to a weekly calendar.

Refer to Figures 4–4 and 4–5.

Daily

Learners should be able to:

- go back to the prioritized set of index cards and identify all the individual steps that had to be done to complete each of the weekly duties (e.g. for preliminary research in the library, such steps as using the library skills worksheet procedure from Chapter 3, taking notes, preparing a graphic organizer, as shown in Figure 4–4);
- using the mnemonic AT WORC, label each of the substeps identified in the weekly step above and transfer this information to a daily calendar or computerized calendar organizer as shown in Figure 4–6.

Refer to Figures 4–4 and 4–6.

Study Time Management

Identifying Time of Day for Studying

In order to use time most effectively to accomplish goals, time-of-day study time management considers at least two aspects of individual behavior. First is to find out when people do their most productive studying or working, and then to organize academic and personal schedules around those times as much as is possible. Second is to consider how to use and structure less productive times for the kind of preliminary library research that does not require the same level of concentration of studying or writing e.g. finding sources and taking rough notes.

Pope (1985) says that most of us, including people with learning disabilities, have a *best* time of day when we can concentrate on quiet activities such as reading and writing. He states that learners should make sure, if at all possible, to schedule activities requiring a clear mind and concentration during those most productive time periods.

Of course, ideal planning is not always possible. But systematically finding out the times in the day when students work most effectively is within all learners' control and provides potentially valuable information for planning and studying.

To discover when these best times occur, suggest that students use a diary to keep track of which time blocks during the day were most effective for in-depth, concentrated work, as opposed to active tasks. Within the confines of personal and family responsibilities, learners can use that information as the basis for daily timetabling planning.

Finding the best time to work is not always practical or possible in occupational training situations. However, trainers and human resource personnel can keep this factor in mind. For example, if training sessions are scheduled at the end of a work day or late shift, the participants may not be able to concentrate. If possible, try to arrange learning activities when people are most alert.

Length of Study Time

Pope (1985) recommends that learning disabled individuals also keep close track, in a diary of some sort, of how long they can concentrate on reading materials or writing tasks. He suggests that they time themselves to discover their pattern of concentration, even if they can only last for a few minutes at first. Learners may end the timing when they note that they are beginning to lose their train of thought or starting to daydream. Instructors and trainers should explain, however, that we all tend to daydream a little to relax and then return to studying. The final cut-off point occurs when students simply cannot get back on task.

Pope also recommends systematically increasing the length of productive work time by four or five minutes at the start of every week. There is no point in moving too fast in this regard because setbacks can occur. If participants are unable to meet their own length-of-study-time schedule they may become frustrated and feel they are failing themselves. Learners should gradually increase their work period to an hour or slightly more; most people cannot concentrate much longer than that without a physical or mental break.

Summary

This chapter has presented some goal-setting and timetabling strategies, as well as study-time management methods and devices. Included has been

discussion of the use of course outlines, index cards, calendars, the mnemonic device "AT WORC," and color coding. All these compensatory supports contribute to teaching learning disabled people *how* to problem-solve,
make decisions, and organize themselves and their educational or occupational responsibilities.

The next chapter outlines a variety of reading fluency and comprehension
compensatory strategies and instructional methods and aids. Also discussed
in Chapter 5 are several multisensory and multidimensional techniques
which contribute to improved understanding of what is read.

5

Reading Fluency and Comprehension

Although people with learning disabilities may share fundamental similarities, they have many different types of reading problems (Johnson 1987b). This chapter outlines the reading process and some strategies for coping with reading fluency and comprehension difficulties.

The Reading Process

Reading is an interactive process. Mayer (1987, 282) explains that every reader has a personal framework for understanding new information, a "schema," to which new pieces of information are linked. Each of us makes meaning from what we read by referring to our previous experiences in our memories. Those experiences are part of a person's schema. Because each person's schema is different from every other person's, several people can read or hear the same passage and yet understand something completely different.

Implicit in both the fluency and comprehension strategies presented in this chapter is a view of the reading process as interactive. This approach makes use of both "bottom-up" and "top-down" reading models. Bottom-up models focus on the perceptual processes of going from the stimulus sensation to some internal representation, e.g. from decoding printed words to comprehending a meaningful sentence. Top-down models focus on the cognitive processes of using one's existing knowledge (i.e. one's internal schema) to impose organization on incoming sensations, e.g. anticipating from context what the next word in a sentence will be. Interactive models, as used herein, focus on both bottom-up perception of visual stimuli and top-down imposition of structure, because both occur simultaneously and interactively (Mayer, 1987, 250).

In this chapter, compensatory strategies are separated into reading fluency and comprehension categories for the sake of both clarity and simplicity of explanation, as well as to match informal or formal assessment data to the most appropriate strategies of instructional techniques. For a more comprehensive explanation of the reading process, practitioners should examine a text devoted to the topic, such as Perfetti, *Reading Ability* (1984).

Automaticity Training For Fluency

Before people can read fluently and for meaning, the underlying basic skills of word decoding and recognition must be automatic. Consider the act of driving and the driver's knowledge of the rules of the road. Anyone who has been a driver for a considerable time remembers the rules only when they are needed, such as to interpret a sign or determine what should be done at the scene of an accident.

Automaticity in reading is similar; good readers do not have to pause to note the individual letters and their sounds in a word in order to recognize each word, nor are they aware of thinking about what each word means in order to extract meaning from a passage of reading material. The following are techniques to increase automaticity.

Repeated Readings

Repeated readings is a strategy for improving automatic decoding skills and compensating for a lack of fluency, accuracy, and attention to meaning. Samuels (1979) explains that fluency greatly improves with repeated readings because the focus, at least initially, is only on finding out what individual words say rather than on understanding the content of the material. In other words, reading the same passages several times leads to increased word recognition as more and more material is first decoded and then remembered. Attention is

Figure 5-1: Overview of Reading Fluency & Comprehension Strategies

LEARNING PROBLEMS	INDIVIDUALIZED STRATEGIES AND SUPPORTS FOR LEARNERS	CLASSROOM METHODS FOR INSTRUCTORS AND TRAINERS
• is unwilling to read	• taped textbooks • DRTA strategy • tutor or peer coach	• special seating arrangements to build confidence
• lacks fluency, accuracy and speed	• taped textbooks and notetaking • repeated readings • verbal rehearsal	• advance organizers on assigned readings or related topics • ConStruct procedure as class activity
• has difficulties sounding out words	• repeated readings • verbal rehearsal • tape recorder and earphones	• ReQuest strategy
• is distractible, loses place on page	• verbal rehearsal • skimming (e.g. with index finger or ruler)	• special arrangements for examinations • special seating arrangements
• does not understand what was read on first reading	• repeated readings • main ideas on index cards • tape recorder and ear phones, plus columnar notetaking strategy • sequential lists	• advance organizers on assigned readings or related topics
• is unable to pick out main ideas, make inferences, or recognize cause and effect relationships	• ConStruct procedure • Multipass strategy • SQ3R strategy • graphic organizers • expand information on index cards	• Multipass as a class activity • graphic or sequential organizers in class
• cannot use contextual cues, access meaning, or integrate sentences	• descriptive organizers, such as concept charting • repeated readings • sustained silent reading	• audiovisual and other methods to cover content of reading
• cannot summarize or synthesize	• self-questioning • tutor or peer coach	• adjunct questions • special arrangements for assignments

directed to word decoding, analysis, and recognition as the individual is allowed time to figure out what is on the page and then reinforce what has been learned by practising the same material again. Eventually, automatic word recognition skills are developed, which allow more attention to be given to meaning.

LaBerge and Samuels (1974) suggest that people with learning disabilities in reading go through three stages in learning to decode text automatically, leaving attention free for processing meaning. They are: (1) an *inaccurate stage*, in which individuals make many errors in word recognition; (2) an *accurate stage*, in which words are recognized but with great effort; and, an *automatic stage*, in which words are recognized correctly without undue attention being required.

Techniques

There are several ways to structure repeated readings so that learners can move from the inaccurate stage through accuracy to automaticity.

- In the classroom, instructors or trainers can arrange activities so that their students have to read an article or text chapter three times. The reason for each reading can be different. For example, the first reading can be for factual information, which is to be presented in a lecture. The second reading can provide the basis for a different session, to discuss what conclusions can be reached. A third and final reading can be followed by ideas for developing recommendations.
- On an individual basis repeated readings can be conducted with a counselor or human resource person. Learners read first into a tape recorder, then listen to their reading using earphones (as they did during HELP) and then read, once more, silently. Alternatively, they can read silently twice and aloud once. The combinations of readings can vary as desired. However, reading material three times is usually enough. It is most important is to tell participants that during the first reading, they are to concentrate only on the words of the passage. They are to wait until the third reading to use comprehension and context cues and to think about meaning. Of course, comprehension is aided when readings are actually taken from classroom activities because learners also will be exposed to instruction on the content.

Rehearsal and Chunking

Rehearsal simply means saying the words and sentences aloud while reading. As we read we all say the words on the page at a subvocal level. However, for individuals with reading problems, especially in automaticity skills, rehearsal is very effective. Interestingly, Flavell, Friedrichs, and Hoyt (1970), as reported in Mayer (1987, 67) find that the spontaneous use of rehearsal strategies increases with age—a good thing for adult educators to know.

The memory device, *chunking*, is a method of aiding recall. Instead of trying to memorize symbols or words individually, they are grouped together. For example, we often learn telephone or social security numbers in sets of two or three, rather than number by number. The childhood alphabet song where the letters are sung in groups is another example. Words and simple phrases can also be memorized in this way.

If a special needs counselor, a literacy tutor, or industrial trainer is working with learners in a one-on-one situation, there are several ways to use rehearsal and chunking strategies, in many combinations. For the most part, however, only people with severe reading deficits need to use rehearsal and chunking strategies on a regular basis.

Reading Comprehension Strategies

Reading For Meaning

Reading for meaning first requires automaticity in decoding and the ability to understand words in a sentence sequence in order to be able to integrate all the information embedded in sentences into an integrated coherent structure. If people with learning disabilities cannot process meaning easily, they usually benefit from multiple organizers and technical aids that help them build on their internal schema.

Tape Recorder and Earphones

A beneficial technique for students who have trouble understanding what they read is to combine the repeated readings strategy with the use of the tape recorder and earphones. This works as well to improve comprehension as it does to improve decoding and fluency.

Participants read their text material into a tape recorder, then listen to what they have taped while taking down short-form notes using a columnar format (see Chapter 6). They next highlight their notes, develop a visual or sequential organizer (Figures 2–3 or 2–4) from their notes, and finally write a summary. This process reflects, of course, the steps of the HELP assessment tool. Reading comprehension is increased because the multiple steps and repetition involved allow for several opportunities to process what is read.

Graphic and Other Organizers

In addition to being part of a multi-dimensional strategy, visual and de-scriptive (sequential) organizers can also be used alone. Some students bene-fit from devising personal organizers every time they read. After taking rough notes during the first reading, they try to create a graphic structure or a point-form list to reflect what they have read. (See Figures 2–3 and 2–4 for examples.) Often, by the time the structure is completed, learners understand what they have read. While this technique is not always effective, it can be very helpful for individuals who can already organize ideas.

Adjunct Questions

For those people with reading problems who cannot yet organize visual or descriptive structures, adjunct questions work well. Adjunct questions re-view the information and implications of material by posing a series of questions to learners on what they have read.

Mayer explains that adjunct questions may serve several purposes, in-cluding directing a reader's attention both forward and backward. *Forward* questions inform readers what to pay attention to and direct notice to certain aspects of the text. *Backward* questions are those that require the reader to review portions of the passage that have already been read (Mayer, 1987, 133). This kind of adjunct questioning can reinforce what learners already know, or pinpoint what they do not understand. The backward technique is

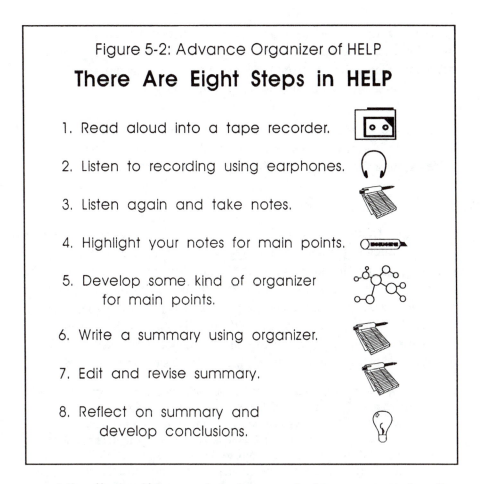

Figure 5-2: Advance Organizer of HELP

There Are Eight Steps in HELP

1. Read aloud into a tape recorder.

2. Listen to recording using earphones.

3. Listen again and take notes.

4. Highlight your notes for main points.

5. Develop some kind of organizer for main points.

6. Write a summary using organizer.

7. Edit and revise summary.

8. Reflect on summary and develop conclusions.

especially effective if learners have been required to use repeated reading and graphic/descriptive organizers prior to adjunct questioning.

By using adjunct questioning instructors and trainers can, therefore, guide reading to help learners understand more clearly. (An advance organizer can work in much the same way (Figure 5–2).)

Multisensory/Multidimensional Strategies

There are other strategies that are interactive and multidimensional as well. They contain several steps or substrategies and can vary in complexity so that instructors and trainers will need to judge carefully which is appropriate for their learners. Some require prerequisite skills, such as the ability to develop flowcharts, as in Figure 2–5. All need to be modeled and practised under the guidance of trainers or counselors. These strategies are multisensory and multidimensional because they involve: seeing, hearing, speaking, thinking, developing diagrams (organizing), surveying and skimming a passage, reading for meaning, summarizing, and developing conclusions.

Special needs personnel and counselors in higher education settings have found the following methods very helpful. They are especially beneficial for students who have already acquired basic research study skills.

The ConStruct Procedure

The word *ConStruct* derives its name from combining parts of the words "concept structuring," and as this suggests is a method of identifying and prioritizing important ideas in what is read. The procedure involves the integration of several readings of a text with the construction of a diagram that depicts the conceptual relationships as readers perceive them (Vaughan, 1984, 130). The approach can be taught for individual use or can be used by instructors and trainers in the classroom as a method for presenting a lecture or discussion on a required reading. There are four steps in the procedure:

- Learners quickly read a selection and pick out the main topic and any subtopics. The purpose of this rapid skimming is for learners to discover as much as they can about the material from the title, subtitle, introductory paragraphs, first sentences of other paragraphs, illustrations, and figures. Once the superordinate concepts have been identified, participants are expected to make up a descriptive and sequential diagram, in much the same fashion as in Figure 2–5. While the diagram contains only the essential or key concepts, it must include enough information to act as a framework for the next three steps.
- The second step involves a thorough reading of the material. Readers are expected to try to understand the meaning of the text but not to attempt to remember everything read. Nonessential information is to be ignored at this point. After finishing the reading task, participants are to add all the essential components to the diagram. At this point the diagram should be much more detailed than in Figure 2–5.
- Before beginning the third and final reading, readers check over their diagram as it now stands. If there is anything they don't understand, they go back and check the reading material for clarification.
- The final reading involves scanning the text for all nonessential data that can clarify or add to what is already on the diagram. That information should be added to the diagram. Once this concept organizer is finished, participants study the diagram to learn all they can about the reading.

The ConStruct Procedure is a very effective multi-dimensional strategy for people in higher education or professional development. The complexity of the diagram's development suggests that the process requires abstract reasoning abilities.

Multipass

Multipass is intended for use in educational or occupational situations which require a lot of reading for those people who need a strategy that allows them to extract enough meaning from material without having to read it thoroughly. Note that this technique can be taught and/or used only with a text that has questions at the end of each chapter, or if adjunct questions are provided by instructors. Multipass is similar to the ConStruct Procedure in many ways, except that learners are not expected to read material thoroughly, and no diagram is required. As with ConStruct, it can be used by individuals or classroom trainers and counselors. There are three substrategies or *passes* in Multipass, as follows (Schumaker, Deshler, Gordon, Warner & Denton, 1982).

- *Survey:* Learners survey or quickly read the text material looking only at titles, subtitles, illustrations, introductory paragraphs, and first sentences of all other paragraphs. Participants may write brief point-form notes.
- *Size-up:* Having first surveyed the reading material, the second step is to size-up or evaluate understanding, using the questions at the end of the chapter, or the adjunct questions provided by instructors, as a guide to what should be understood. The purpose of this step is to help learners get as much from the reading as possible, without having to read it from start to finish. Any new material or insights can be added to the brief notes taken during the survey stage.
- *Sorting-out:* Sorting out involves reviewing the notes written and trying to answer the questions provided. If participants still cannot answer a question, or part of a question, they go back to the reading and find the appropriate answer. Once learners can answer all of the questions, they have successfully completed the strategy.

SQ3R

As with the two previous techniques, SQ3R is a tool designed to help learners read faster, with more accuracy, and acquire more meaning. The letters stand for the three steps or *passes* to be completed: (1) survey S; (2) question Q; and (3) read, recite, and review 3R (Adams, Carnine & Gersten, 1982).

Pass One: (S)

Learners quickly survey (S) the reading material. As with Multipass, they take note of titles, subtitles, illustrations, etc. to get a general sense of the reading.

Pass Two: (Q), (R1), (R2)

During the second pass, participants take all of the subtitles and turn them into questions (Q). They are then expected to read (R1) the passage so that they can answer each of their own questions. Once they can write an answer for each question, they rehearse their answers by reciting (R2) them aloud.

Pass Three: (R3)

The final pass consists of a wrap-up review (R3) of the reading passage. By now learners should be able to discuss the reading material and write a short summary based on the answers to their own questions completed during the second pass.

DRTA

DRTA, which stands for *D*irected *R*eading and *T*hinking *A*ctivity, also involves three steps: (1) predict; (2) read; and (3) prove (Stauffer, 1975). It can be fun, as well as aid comprehension, and can be used in large classroom situations or in small discussion groups.

- *Predict.* First, instructors display a picture or read a few sentences from one section of a required reading. Learners then try to guess (predict) what that part of the text is or will be about.
- *Read and Prove.* The second and third steps are carried out concurrently. After guessing what the passage is about, students read the applicable passage carefully, trying to find evidence to support their predictions. The process is continued in the same way for each separate section of text.

For example, if the reading is a research paper, each section would be covered separately: (1) the abstract; (2) the introduction; (3) the review of the literature; (4) the method and procedures; (5) the results; (6) the conclusions; and (7) recommendations. Or, in industry, each section of a shop manual would be discussed in the same manner. Questions and predictions might cover product safety procedures, accident prevention, fire safety, fire prevention, long-term disability, and so on.

ReQuest

ReQuest is an effective strategy in small groups or in one-on-one learning situations. Both instructors and learners read a passage silently, and then ask each other questions about what they have read. Mayer (1987, 308) states that this procedure is helpful in teaching participants how to formulate questions, as well as leading to better understanding of the reading material.

Summary

This chapter has discussed the reading process (i.e. the role of a reader's internal schema and reading as an interactive process), automaticity training for improving reading fluency and reading comprehension strategies. To help people with learning disabilities in reading, a variety of compensatory methods were suggested, including repeated readings, rehearsal and chunking procedures, and use of tape recorders and earphones. Other techniques, intended to increase the likelihood of people understanding what they have read, were presented. Some of the reading comprehension strategies, such as using a tape recorder and graphic organizers, are similar to the automaticity training suggestions. Adjunct questioning and several multisensory and multidimensional procedures were also outlined. Although some of these reading strategies seem complex, they may offer benefits to individuals with learning problems. Even if improvement is only marginal, the effort involved for both instructor and student will be worth it.

Chapter 6 discusses notetaking strategies, including columnar formats, signaling, advance organizers, and using tape recorders and earphones in yet another context. Also included in the next chapter are written language strategies that help individuals with learning disabilities improve their prose writing skills.

6
Notetaking and Written Language

Functional illiteracy, the inability to read and write adequately, is one of the most vexing problems in continuing and industrial education today. The ability to organize thoughts clearly and present them in coherent and grammatical written form is essential in most school courses. And shop manuals and safety programs assume that personnel have basic reading and writing skills. Thus, written language problems can seriously limit educational and occupational opportunities for learning disabled adults. Their writing is both visible and permanent, leaving the faulty results as a constant reminder of their problems.

As will become obvious throughout this chapter, writing requires that people be able to do much more than simply read and record words on the printed page. Many intellectual abilities are involved. In childhood, unless normal development is interrupted, children first develop auditory receptive language, then oral expressive language, then reading skills, and, finally, expressive language in the form of writing. While writing is the skill at the apex of the reading, writing hierarchy and is dependent on successful acquisition of preceding skills, it is important to realize that, just as with reading, all of these skills and abilities are interactive; they are not learned or used in a linear fashion (Johnson, 1987c).

This final chapter is divided into two sections in which the skills and strategies required for writing text (first part) and taking notes (second part) in the classroom are outlined. Within each of the sections, the following

Figure 6-1: Overview of Notetaking and Written Language Strategies

LEARNING PROBLEMS	INDIVIDUALIZED STRATEGIES AND SUPPORTS FOR LEARNERS	CLASSROOM METHODS FOR INSTRUCTORS AND TRAINERS
• handwriting is illegible	• tape recorder and earphones • microcomputer and word processing program	• course handouts • notetakers
• cannot stay on line	• microcomputer and word processing program	
• has difficulty copying letters or words	• tape recorder • graphic organizers	• special arrangements for assignments and examinations
• writes and prints in same assignment	• tape recorder and earphones • microcomputer and word processing program	• special arrangements for assignments and examinations
• writing is slow	• tape recorder and earphones to take notes	• audiovisual equipment
• omits capital letters and punctuation	• diary for self-monitoring • special needs or individual counseling • peer tutors	
• cannot write grammatically	• special needs or individual counseling • typing and editorial services • peer tutors • sentence combining	
• has severe spelling problems	• use of the Horn method • peer tutors • electronic computerized dictionaries • special needs or individual counseling and diary of errors/ corrections • use of alphabetized index cards • editorial services	• highlighting errors when evaluating written work
• spells same word different ways	• microcomputer with spellcheck program • diary for self-monitoring	
• cannot use dictionary	• special needs or individual counseling	

Figure 6-1: Overview of Notetaking and Written Language Strategies (Continued)		
LEARNING PROBLEMS	**INDIVIDUALIZED STRATEGIES AND SUPPORTS FOR LEARNERS**	**CLASSROOM METHODS FOR INSTRUCTORS AND TRAINERS**
• has difficulties developing graphic organizers for pre-writing planning	• sequence lists (point-form) • sequence charting • peer tutors • special needs or individual counseling	• graphic organizers for lectures and examination questions • advance organizers for class work
• cannot select main ideas to include in written assignments	• graphic organizers • sequence lists • signaling/highlighting • sentence combining • use of index cards	• graphic organizers for class work • advance organizers to show progress
• has difficulty putting sentences and paragraphs together	• sentence combining • peer tutors • graphic organizers such as sequence charting • use of index cards or large chart paper and markers	• feedback on assignments
• has problems reviewing, editing, and self-monitoring written text	• signaling/highlighting • microcomputer and word processor spellcheck • tape recorder and earphones • peer tutors • editing services	• feedback on assignments • refer to advisor or for counseling
• pays little or no attention to layout, spacing, or indentation	• peer tutors • typing and editing services	• modeling in class
• cannot retain information heard in a classroom	• tape recorder • columnar notetaking • signaling/highlighting	• audiovisual and multiple methods of presentation
• has difficulty deciding what to include in meeting or lecture notes	• graphic organizers • point-form lists • signaling/highlighting	• graphic organizers for class activities • point-form display on overhead projector • advance organizers to show topics to be covered • identification of what is most and least important

strategies and aids that can help or compensate for learning difficulties related to writing will be outlined:

- graphic organizers;
- sequence and concept charting;
- microcomputers;
- the Horn spelling method;
- tape-recording equipment;
- sentence combining;
- diaries;
- the "Editwrite" method for editing written expression;
- advance organizers;
- columnar notetaking formats; and,
- signaling and highlighting.

All of these methods, their relationship to specific types of learning problems, and who can help, are presented in Figure 6–1.

The Writing Process

The *writing process* model presented in this chapter provides counselors,
instructors, and trainers with a systematic framework for teaching people
with learning disabilities the various compensatory strategies and technical
aids that can help them learn to write. The model consists of three separate
steps or processes: (1) planning, (2) translating (writing) and (3) reviewing
(Bruce, Collins, Rubin & Gentner, 1982; Hayes & Flower, 1980; Nold,
1981).

Within each of these major steps of planning, writing, and reviewing are
other shorter processes, requiring a separate set of skills and involving more
compensatory strategies. For example, to be able to plan what to write, one
must be able to retrieve, select, and organize information. Translating or
writing and reviewing are equally complex and involve aspects such as
vocabulary, grammar, sentence combining, spelling, penmanship, and self-
monitoring. Is it any wonder that learning disabled people struggle with the
writing process?

While the planning process can be carried out in the classroom, due to the
individualized nature of the writing and reviewing process, the methods and

activities suggested for those stages are usually best completed on an individual basis with a tutor or under the supervision of a special needs or human resource counselor. Nevertheless, instructors and trainers need to be aware of these strategies and aids in order to make more accurate referrals, and to provide their learners with the feedback that is most appropriate to their needs and performance.

Planning

No matter what the learning setting, purpose for writing, or format required, planning to write is a complex interactive process involving several skills and abilities. Learners must be able to:

- retrieve and process information from long-term memory;
- process new information and integrate it with what is already known;
- select and prioritize what is most important, least important, and what can be eliminated from the available information;
- develop a writing plan; and
- establish criteria for implementing that plan.

A variety of graphic or descriptive organizers and charts can help people work through this complex process. (This technique was also mentioned in Chapter 5, during discussion of the ConStruct Procedure, as a means of improving reading comprehension.)

Graphic and Sequential Organizers

Graphic organizers are a compensatory strategy for people who have difficulties with generating, organizing, or selecting, ideas. The word *graphic* describes the format of this technique—a method of organizing material in *pictorial* form. It thus provides learners with a "picture" or simultaneous presentation of information, making it easier for them to decide what has to be written, what connections exist among the ideas, and in what order those ideas should be recorded. This technique can be used effectively in either classroom situations or counseling sessions.

Four types of graphic organizers are presented in this chapter: (1) flowcharts, (2) imagery maps, (3) concept charts, and (4) sequence charts. For examples of a flowchart and imagery map, see Figures 2–2, 2–4, 2–5, and

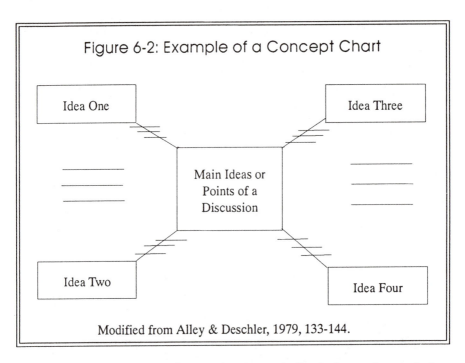

Figure 6-2: Example of a Concept Chart

Idea One

Idea Three

Main Ideas or
Points of a
Discussion

Idea Two

Idea Four

Modified from Alley & Deschler, 1979, 133-144.

2–6. in Chapter 2. Sequential organizers are similar in intent, but their formats tend to be descriptive, hierarchical, interrelated, and successive. See Figure 6–2, for a concept chart centred on a main idea, and Figure 6–3, for a sequence chart based on a time sequence, as the focus around which all other ideas are connected.

Learning disabled people often benefit from developing more than one type of organizer for each writing task. For example, a library study skills procedure and worksheet for gathering preliminary research information was presented in Chapter 3. Whether used in higher education, or modified for an occupational setting, the results of that kind of pre-planning can be recorded on a flowchart. In effect, the preliminary research is the first step of the writing process. The second step generates information from the research process by itemizing facts in a simple point-form descriptive list. Once this list is complete, it is helpful to go back over the various points. Learners can either prioritize and sequence the facts and ideas or group them together where appropriate. In the final steps, participants make a sequence or graphic flowchart or imagery map showing how all the ideas and facts are related, and organize this information into an action plan. Index cards and/or large chart paper is useful for recording each list and diagram, while color coding helps clarify the various connections and relationships among ideas.

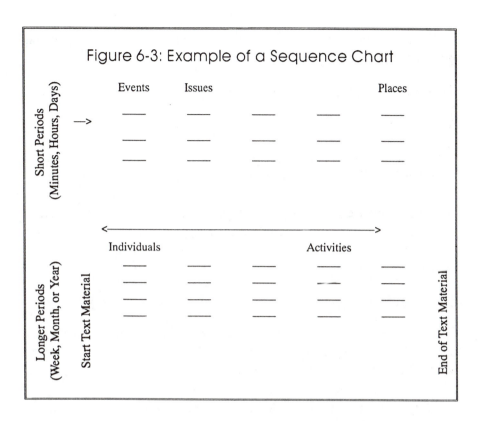

Figure 6-3: Example of a Sequence Chart

In Chapter 1 the differences between visual, auditory, and shallow learning styles and the types of strategies and tactics preferred by people when learning and working were noted. Visual strategies, such as flowcharting and imagery mapping, are excellent techniques for those who demonstrate a visual learning preference because they are able to see all the information simultaneously. However, for those whose learning style preference is auditory, it is advisable to use additional methods, such as sequential and prioritized lists. Using both simultaneous and sequential techniques can be very effective for all learners because their learning style preference is reinforced while their weaker style is strengthened. Thus, a combination of both of these multisensory methods and strategies often is more effective than using visual or sequential methods alone for instruction in either reading or written language.

A more detailed discussion of the four steps involved in the planning process now follows.

The Pre-writing Steps (in pencil)

Step One

Learners develop an itemized point-form list, and/or a series of index cards from their sources of preliminary information, such as research study worksheets in an educational setting, or meetings, manuals, and training sessions in industrial training situations. While devising such sequential methods is often difficult in this early planning stage, the process encourages participants to think about where they are heading and what they must do at each step of the way.

Step Two

Using these preliminary methods, participants with a predominately visual cognitive learning style consult their available sources of information, as well as recall as much material as possible, to generate a graphic organizer. As with brainstorming, at this stage information is written down without deciding whether or not it should be used. People with an auditory sequential learning style preference may simply keep their point-form list and/or index cards, or they may develop a graphic organizer to complement this first method.

Step Three

After the list or graphic organizer is finished, learners should reread it and prioritize and sequence items. They must now make decisions about what will be included or eliminated in their writing and make additions or revisions as necessary.

Step Four

The final task of planning is to write up an *action plan* based on the flowchart and/or the prioritized list.

Action Plan

This is an example of an *action plan* for a psychology essay on child development. Remember that the action plan would be devised only *after* the point-form list and graphic and/or sequential organizers have already been developed and revised.

1. *Introduction:* to include the points to be discussed in the body of the paper; for example, understanding Piaget's theory of child development and why that knowledge may be important.

2. *Body of Essay:* develop the ideas in detail. For example:
   * Outline major features of Piaget's theory in brief (Mayer, 1987, 21-23):
     − relative, functional, dialectical, intrinsic stages.
   * Discuss changes in the child's representation of objects and the four stages or periods and ages at transition:
     − sensorimotor, preoperational, concrete operations, formal operations.
   * Include examples of object accomplishment:
     − object permanence, object conservation.
   * Expand on major features when describing examples of object accomplishment at the various stages: e.g.
     − relative (all cognitive growth realtive to existing knowledge);
     − functional (adaptation continually requires more information while internal organization reduces complexity to the development stage);
     − dialectical (the opposing processes of assimilation and accommodation);
     − instrinsic (assimilation of information that is slightly more complex into the cognitive system).

3. *Summary and Conclusions:*
   * Make sure the summary is consistent with what is stated in the introduction. If not, make necessary changes.
   * Explain the importance of any conclusions.
     − E.g. Why is an awareness of child development important, and to whom? Point out that it is important for child-care workers, parents, and teachers when teaching children and planning curriculum and activities so that what the children do and learn is at the appropriate developmental level, as well as knowing when and how to challenge a child's learning.

Other Uses of Graphic Organizers

Graphic organizers can be extremely effective in other types of pre-writing situations:

- to review course content prior to a test or formal examination;
- to summarize or provide a framework for a lecture and notetaking; and,
- to provide the basis for creating or answering examination questions.

In the latter case, organizers can be used in at least two ways:

- instructors and trainers ask learners to develop examination questions from their diagrams, and then answer their own questions; or,
- educators include a compulsory question for which the diagram or chart acts as a visual or sequential organizer of the answer to the question.

Writing

The ideas expressed visually on flowcharts, imagery maps, or sequential lists and charts in the first stage of writing must now be "translated" into written form. In the context of the writing process outlined here, translating means producing a written text that is consistent with the *action plan.*

This second stage requires learners to interpret the visual information on their charts and convey it in sentences and paragraphs. This is actually the first draft stage of formal writing, which involves writing, revising, and rewriting.

Producing a written text requires a series of skills, many of which are lacking in people with learning difficulties. For example, a knowledge of the rules of grammar and spelling are essential. In addition, to write, people must be able to produce properly formed letters and symbols; some individuals' handwriting is illegible or difficult to understand.

Some techniques and technical equipment that can be used to aid writing:

- a microcomputer/word processor with a spellcheck feature;
- an electronic computerized device with a dictionary data card;
- the Horn spelling method;

- a list of common spelling mistakes;
- a tape recorder and earphones; and,
- sentence combining.

Microcomputers with Spellcheck

If learners have the requisite typing and computer skills, microcomputers with word processing programs can help in many ways. They can compensate for both illegible handwriting and poor spelling skills. People with learning disabilities often lack self-monitoring skills necessary for detection or correction of error (Johnson, 1987c). Most word processing programs have a spellcheck feature that can significantly reduce spelling errors. Some electronic typewriters have a feature that stops individuals as soon as they have typed an error. However, in order to use any of these aids, students must be able to recognize the correct version of the word or supply it themselves.

The Horn Spelling Method

One study method for helping participants deal with their spelling deficits is the Horn Spelling Method. This is a step-by-step approach for learning how to spell unfamiliar or misspelled words. The steps are as follows (Polloway, Patton, Payne, & Payne, 1989, 265):

- Pronounce each word carefully as you write or type it.
- Look carefully at each part of the word as you pronounce it.
- Say the letters in sequence.
- Attempt to recall how the word looks, then spell it aloud.
- Write the word if that is necessary to remember it.
- Repeat the above steps if required.

Common Spelling Mistakes

In conjunction with the Horn spelling method, it may be useful to provide learners with a list of spelling rules. Some of the most frequent errors occur as failures to observe rules in the following situations:

- Remembering silent letters such as "k" "p" "h" and "t," e.g. knife, pneumonia, character, match;
- Removing the "e" when adding "ing," e.g. hike, hiking;
- Doubling a final consonant when adding "ing," e.g. putting, sitting;
- Including the long vowel "e" following "t" "k" "g" and "v," e.g. skate, bake, stage, gave;

- Correctly spelling vowel pairs such as "ea" "ou" and "ie," e.g. eat, out, piece;
- Using "a" or "an" correctly before a word, e.g. a house, an opening;
- Confusing "as" with "has."

Tape Recorders and Handwriting

Although computers can be used to compensate for poor handwriting, for those who cannot write at all, the tape recorder and earphones are additional necessary compensatory devices. Participants use their sequential lists, flowcharts, or image maps in the usual way, as the basis for what they want included in a written text. But, instead of writing, they translate their flowcharts into words by *dictating* what they want to say directly into a tape recorder. Later, using earphones, they type the material on the tape into their computers. Further changes and corrections are made on screen as well.

Sentence Combining

Combining sentences is an extremely effective strategy for people who need help in composing coherent sentences and paragraphs.

- Learners return to the prioritized list completed during the planning stage. For *each* item or entry on that list, learners write one or more sentences on small index cards. If possible every sentence is written on a separate card. Cut the index cards in half or thirds, if necessary, to have one card for every sentence. Participants are informed that sentences do not have to be written in any kind of order, just that all necessary ideas and information must be recorded before moving on to the next item.
- When all the sentences are written, learners group all the index cards or pieces of cards according to category or topic.
- After all the sentences are categorized and grouped according to topic or idea, participants must prioritize ideas by logically arranging which sentence should come first, second, and so on. This is done for each separate category or topic.
- Participants are now ready to put sentences together. They simply begin with the first sentence in the first category and then continue until all the sentences are combined into one continuous essay.
- When all the sentences have been brought together, each of the individual categories can be separated into paragraphs. Usually, it will be necessary to compose other paragraphs within each topic area as well.
- For individuals with handwriting difficulties, sentences are typed on a computer, printed out, and then arranged in the same way. Com-

bining sentences can then be done on the computer, or they can be dictated into a tape recorder and transcribed later.

Reviewing

To be able to review and correct one's own work requires reading and self-monitoring skills. Mayer (1987, 303) refers to this process as metacognition. Mayer says that a reader with good comprehension monitoring skills continually asks "Does this make sense?" The writer must ask the same question to ensure that meaning is being conveyed.

Learners also need to be able to monitor the technical components of written expression, such as grammar, capitalization, punctuation, and spelling.

Using a Diary/Index Cards

A diary is a useful device for learners with self-monitoring problems. They record their concerns as they are writing; for example, Do sentences make sense? Are words correctly used? Are ideas adequately expressed? Is spacing and layout correct? Are citations correct? They also keep track of any concerns or questions about spelling, punctuation, and capitalization. Participants keep the diary handy as they review each sentence and make note of all possible problems. This diary can be used effectively by those who frequently misspell words. For example, misspelled words and corrected versions can be listed, added to as required, and used as a resource during the reviewing process. Index cards and a file box can also be used, but with the added advantage that the errors/corrections can be entered in alphabetical order for quick reference. In addition both the list of spelling rules in the previous translating section and the "Editwrite" capitalization and punctuation rules to follow will help learners correct their work.

Technical Equipment

The spellcheck feature on word processing programs or electronic type-writers is helpful for reviewing work already completed.

A tape recorder can be used for reviewing as well. Learners slowly and carefully record everything they have written. Later, they listen to what they have written with earphones. If anything doesn't make sense, they know they must make revisions.

If a word processor is used, sentences which have been dictated into a tape recorder and then transcribed into the computer can be revised when viewed on the computer monitor.

Editwrite Format for Editing

Editwrite has been the name of my private practice to counsel others on how to write and edit what they have written. The "Editwrite" format is intended to help learners edit "right." It involves two lists of rules: one for correct punctuation, and the other for capitalization. These are the rules that are most frequently broken.

What to Capitalize:

- The first word in a sentence.
- The first word in a direct quotation that is itself a complete sentence.
- The first word of every line of poetry.
- Proper names.
- The pronoun "I."
- Titles of office or rank before names, such as Prime Minister or President.
- Department titles in education or employment.
- Geographical terms such as countries, regions, provinces, states, and cities.
- Official names of specific buildings and public places, such as schools, parks, government departments.
- Street names.
- The days of the week and months of the year, holidays and holy days.
- Titles of books, poems, newspapers, journals, articles, plays, films, and songs.
- Course titles or subjects.
- Abbreviations such as St., Rd., Mr., and Dr.
- Trade names of manufactured products unless they have been established as common nouns (e.g. aspirin).

Where Punctuation is Required:

- A period after a statement.
- Periods after initials, for people or places.
- Periods after abbreviations, such as Mr., Dr., and Ave.
- Question marks after an interrogatory expression (a question) (?).
- Exclamation mark after a strong statement (!).
- Quotation marks before and after a direct quote or words or short phrases that need to stand out ("..."). Also be used to identify magazine and journal articles (i.e., parts of a published work such as a book, magazine, or journal). (The title of the book, magazine, or journal is underlined or put into italics.)

- Comma between the day of the month and the year; street address and city; city and state or province; e.g. September 1, 1991; 24 Sussex Drive, Ottawa, Ontario K1M 1M4.
- Comma to separate items in a series of three or more; e.g. People need practise with spelling, punctuation, and capitalization.
- Comma or period at end of quotation marks.
- Colon to separate hours and minutes; e.g. 9:00 am.
- Colon to introduce a list or series.
- Apostrophe to show possession; e.g. the child's toys.
- Hyphen in numbers and compound words; e.g. twenty-one, mother-in-law.

Notetaking

Notetaking provides a means to guide attention and retrieve information from long-term memory so that learners can make connections between what they already know and have experienced with what they are hearing. Notetaking also provides opportunities for participants to separate what is important from what is unimportant.

Saski, Swicegood, and Carter (1983, 269-270) say that notetaking can best be described as an individualized process of organizing information into a usable format that is dependent on active student participation. Specifically, notetaking requires that learners be able simultaneously to:

- listen;
- recognize main ideas and connections;
- concentrate on content; and,
- organize all of the above.

Usually, notetaking is assumed to be strictly the responsibility of students; however, instructors and trainers also bear a major responsibility. As Aaronson, (1975, 11) suggests, notetaking does not occur in a vacuum; the quality of notes taken is affected by the student's familiarity with the subject and the lecturer's teaching style. A confused, rambling, or discursive lecture is decidedly more difficult to record and organize than a well-sequenced lecture.

Some techniques instructors can use to improve students' notetaking skills are:

- to use an advance organizer and follow the items in sequence as shown on it;

Figure 6-4: Two-column Notetaking Format

Recording Lecture Notes in Short Form	Summarizing Facts and Conclusions

- to tell participants when something is important and should be noted;
- to mention when something is irrelevant and should not be included in their notes;
- to review each main point before going on to a new item;
- to pause during lectures and discussions to allow for sufficient writing time;
- to use adjunct questioning (see Chapter 5) to guide learners' notetaking, as well as comprehension of course readings; and,
- to ask the students to review the lecture or discussion at the end of the class period, even if only briefly, so that they can add any additional information, cues, or questions.

Notetaking Formats

There are many columnar formats for recording lecture or other classroom notes. Most consist of two or three columns. All provide wide space for taking notes, with narrow spaces for minor points, supporting informa-

Figure 6-5: Three-Column Notetaking Format

Recording Lecture Notes in Short Form	Summarizing Facts and Conclusions	Information Related to Reading or Assignments

tion, summaries, or student questions and study cues (cf. Alley & Deshler, 1979, 134-136). (See Figures 6–4 and 6–5.) Most learners prefer the two-column style because it allows more room for the summary.

Advance Organizers

An advance organizer is information that is provided in advance by the instructor which can be used by students to organize and interpret lecture or discussion notes by building external connections with existing knowledge (Mayer, 1987, 121–122). For example, Figure 5–2 (see Chapter 5) was developed as an advance organizer for workshops on the HELP informal assessment method (see Chapter 2). Each of the HELP steps is outlined in sequence, with a small diagram beside each step to represent that step. Using both images or words makes it helpful for learners with either a visual or auditory learning style preference.

Advance organizers work best when learners either do not possess or would not normally use appropriate prerequisite knowledge for organizing incoming information. In other words, they work very well for participants who lack prior knowledge (Mayer, 1987, 120-125).

Signaling/Highlighting

When using notetaking formats, signaling techniques, such as using a highlighter pen or underlining, are useful to identify important new information and make connections among the various points in notes. Signaling is especially useful if one of the narrow columns is to be used to write a short summary. Just as highlighting can be used as a guide to devising a framework for a graphic or sequencing organizer prior to writing a summary, it can be used before summarizing notes.

As soon as possible after a lecture or training session, participants decide on a signaling method and use it to identify all the main ideas or relevant points in their lecture notes. Whether using a two- or three-column format, the notetaking and subsequent signaling is done in the widest column. Following the completion of signaling, learners write a summary of five or six sentences in the narrow column. It is also a good idea for participants to add a short statement that shows some evidence of critical reflection, such as conclusions based on the information presented in the lecture.

Recapitulation of Notetaking Strategies

A catchy mnemonic to help instructors, trainers, and counselors remember the important points about notetaking is to think of the "5 R's" (Deese & Deese, 1979):

- *r*ecording;
- *r*educing;
- *r*eciting;
- *r*eflecting; and,
- *r*eviewing .

Using the three-column format (Figure 6–5), the widest column provides space to *r*ecord the notes. Once the lecture notes have been completed, learners use a signaling technique to *r*educe the main ideas. Using these main ideas, a summary and concluding statement is written in the designated narrow column; then learners repeat the sentences subvocally or aloud. These tasks integrate the concepts in the final *R*'s, *r*eciting, *r*eflecting and *r*eviewing.

Summary

Writing process and notetaking strategies, skills, and formats that can be used as compensatory strategies for adults with learning disabilities have been outlined in this chapter. A variety of strategies and devices are necessary in order to develop a plan of action, translate that plan into writing, and review the results. Some instructional techniques were also outlined that can improve learners' chances to take effective notes.

Where Do We Go From Here?

Like people who are not learning disabled, not all learning disabled people wish to change or try something new. This reluctance can be due to many factors, such as a lack of motivation or perseverance, or a fear of change on the part of either learners or educators. Or problems may arise at school and at work from lack of knowledge about learning disabilities and how to help those who suffer from them. This book has attempted to provide some of that knowledge and know-how.

Whether in educational, occupational, or social settings, it is my sincere hope that this book will provide informal assessment know-how and compensatory techniques that will increase the chance for adults with learning disabilities to realize their potential and reach the goals they set for themselves.

References

Aaronson, S.

1975   Notetaking improvement: A combined auditory, functional and psychological approach. *Journal of Reading*, 19 (1), 8-12.

Adams, A., D. Carnine, & R. Gerstsen

1982   Instructional strategies for studying content area texts in the intermediate grades. *Reading Research Quarterly*, 18, 27-55.

Alley, G.R., & D.D. Deshler

1979   *Teaching the Learning Disabled Adolescent: Strategies and Methods*. Denver, CO: Love Publishing.

Anderson, J.R.

1985   *Cognitive Psychology and its Implications*, 2nd ed. San Francisco, CA: W.H. Freeman.

Bachor, D. G., & C. Crealock

1986   *Instructional Strategies for Students with Special Needs*. Englewood Cliffs, NJ: Prentice-Hall.

Barnett, J.E., F.J. DiVesta, & J.T. Rogozinski

1981   What is learned in notetaking? *Journal of Educational Psychology*, 73, 181-192.

Blalock, J.W.

1981   Persistent problems and concerns of young adults with learning disabilities. In A. Silver, ed., *Bridges to Tomorrow: Selected papers from the 17th International Conference of the*

Association for Children With Learning Disabilities. Syracuse, NY: Syracuse University Press.

1987   Auditory language disorders. In D.J. Johnson & J.W. Blalock, eds., *Adults With Learning Disabilities.* Orlando, FL: Grune & Stratton.

Blalock, J.W., & D.J. Johnson

1987   Primary concerns and group characteristics. In D.J.Johnson & J.W. Blalock, eds., *Adults With Learning Disabilities.* Orlando, FL: Grune & Stratton.

Bruce,B., A. Collins, A. Rubin, & D. Gentner.

1982.   Three perspectives on writing. *Educational Psychologist,* 17, 131-145.

Brundage, D., & D. Mackeracher

1980   *Adult Learning Principles and their Application to Program Planning.* Toronto, ON: Ontario Institute for Studies in Education.

Bursuck, W.D., E. Rose, S. Cowen, & M.A. Yahaya

1989   Nationwide survey of postsecondary education services for students with learning disabilities. *Exceptional Children,* 56 (3), 236-245.

Cafforella, R.S., & E.P. Caffarella

1986   Self-directedness and learning contracts in adult education. *Adult Education Quarterly,* 36 (4), 226–234.

Case, R.

1985   *Intellectual Development: Birth to Adulthood.* Orlando, FL: Academic Press.

Cranton, P.

1989   *Planning Instruction for Adult Learners.* Toronto, ON: Wall & Emerson, Inc.

Crux, S.C., & G.P. O'Neill

1988   Curricular interventions for LD students in a university continuing education program. *Canadian Journal of University Continuing Education,* 14 (2), 50-67.

Deese, J., & E. Deese

1979   *How to Study.* New York, NY: McGraw-Hill.

Flavell, J.H., A.G. Friedrichs, & J.D. Hoyt

1970   Developmental changes in memorization processes. *Cognitive Psychology*, 1, 324-340.

Gagne, R.M.

1977   *The Conditions of Learning*, 3rd. ed. New York, NY: Holt, Rinehart and Winston.

1987   *Instructional Technology: Foundations.* Hillsdale, NJ: Lawrence Erlbaum Associates, Publishers.

Hammill, D.D., J.E. Leigh, G. McNutt, & S.C. Larsen

1981   A new definition of learning disabilities. *Learning Disability Quarterly*, 4, 336-341.

Hayes, J.R., & L.S. Flower

1980   Identifying the organization of writing processes. In L.W. Gregg & E.R. Steinberg, eds., *Cognitive Processes in Writing*. Hillsdale, NJ: Lawrence Erlbaum Associates, Publishers.

Holley, C.D., & D.F. Dansereau

1984   The development of spatial learning strategies. In C.D. Holley & D.F. Dansereau, eds., *Spatial Learning Strategies: Techniques, Applications, and Related Issues.* Orlando, FL: Academic Press.

Hollingsworth, P.M., & D.R. Reutzel

1988   Whole language with LD children. *Academic Therapy*, 23 (5), 477-487.

Johnson, D.J.

1987a   Principles of assessment and diagnosis. In D.J. Johnson & J.W. Blalock, eds., *Adults With Learning Disabilities.* Orlando, FL: Grune & Stratton.

1987b   Reading disabilities. In D.J. Johnson & J.W. Blalock, eds., *Adults With Learning Disabilities.* Orlando, FL: Grune & Stratton.

1987c   Disorders of written language. In D.J. Johnson & J.W. Blalock, eds., *Adults With Learning Disabilities*. Orlando, FL: Grune & Stratton.

Johnson, D.J., & J.W. Blalock, eds.

1987a   *Adults With Learning Disabilities*. Orlando, FL: Grune & Stratton.

1987b   Summary of problems and needs. In D.J. Johnson & J.W. Blalock, eds., *Adults With Learning Disabilities*. Orlando, FL: Grune & Stratton.

Kemp, J.E.

1985   *The Instructional Design Process*. Philadelphia, PA: Harper and Row.

Knowles, M.S.

1986   *Using Learning Contracts*. San Francisco, CA: Jossey-Bass.

1989   Learning after retirement. *Adult Learning*, 1 (3), 8–10.

Kolb, D.A.

1984   *Experiential Learning: Experience as the Source of Learning and Development*. Englewood Cliffs, NJ: Prentice-Hall.

Kronick, D., & C. Smith

1988   *Toward Productive Living*. Ottawa, ON: Learning Disabilities Association of Canada.

Kuhl, P.

1982   Speech perception: An overview of current issues. In N. Lass, L. McReynolds, J. Northern, & D. Yoder, eds., *Speech, Language and Hearing*, Vol. 1. Philadelphia, PA: W.B. Saunders.

LaBerge, D., & S.J. Samuels

1974   Toward a theory of automatic information processing in reading. *Cognitive Psychology*, 6, 293-323.

Luria, A.

1966   *Human Brain and Psychological Processes*. New York, NY: Harper and Row.

Masland, R.

1976   The advantages of being dyslexic. *Bulletin of the Orton Dyslexia Society*, 26, 10-18.

Mayer, R.E.

1987   *Educational Psychology: A Cognitive Approach*. Boston, MA: Little, Brown and Co.

1988   Learning strategies: An overview. In C.E. Weinstein, E.T. Goetz, & P.A. Alexander, eds., *Learning and study strategies*. Orlando, FL: Academic Press.

Mezirow, J.

1977   Perspective transformation. *Studies in Adult Education*, 9, 100-110.

1981   A critical theory of adult learning and education. *Adult Education*, 32 (1), 3-24.

Michaels, C.

1986   Increasing faculty awareness and cooperation: Procedures for assisting college students with learning disabilities. In *Charting the Course: Directions in Higher Education for Disabled Students*. Columbus, OH: Association of Handicapped Student Services and Programs in Post-secondary Education.

Nold, E.W.

1981   Revising. In C.H. Frederiksen & J.F. Dominic, eds., *Writing: Volume 2*. Hillsdale, NJ: Lawrence Erlbaum Associates, Publishers.

Norman, D.A.

1982   *Learning and Memory*. San Francisco, CA: W.H. Freeman.

Ochs, E., & B. Schieffelin

1979   *Developmental pragmatics*. New York, NY: Academic Press.

Perfetti, C.A.

1984   *Reading Ability*. New York, NY: Oxford University Press.

Polloway, E.A., J.R. Patton, J.S. Payne, & R.A. Payne

1989   *Strategies for Teaching Learners with Special Needs*, Fourth Edition. Columbus, OH: Merrill.

Pope, S.

1985   Counselling the learning disabled. *Guidance and Counselling,* 1 (2), 27–32.

Rogers, C.R.

1969   *Freedom to Learn.* Columbus, OH: Merrill Publishing.

Samuels, S.J.

1979   The method of repeated readings. *The Reading Teacher,* 32, 403-408.

Saski, J., P. Swicegood, & J.Carter

1983   Notetaking formats for learning disabled adolescents. *Learning Disabilities Quarterly,* 6, 265-272.

Schmeck, R.R.

1988   Individual differences and learning strategies. In C.E. Weinstein, E.T. Goetz, & P.A. Alexander, eds., *Learning and Study Strategies.* Orlando, FL: Academic Press.

Schumaker, J.B., D.D. Deshler, G.R. Alley, & M.M. Warner

1983   Toward the development of an intervention model for learning disabled adolescents. *Exceptional Education Quarterly,* 4 (1), 45-74.

Schumaker, J.B., D.D. Deshler, G.R. Gordon, M.M. Warner, & P.H. Denton

1982   Multipass: A learning strategy for improving reading comprehension. *Learning Disability Quarterly,* 5, 295-304.

Snow, R.E.

1989   Toward assessment of cognitive and conative structures in learning. *Educational Researcher,* 18 (9), 8-14.

Stauffer, R.G.

1975   *Directing the Reading-thinking Process.* New York, NY: Harper & Row.

Stone, C.A.

1987   Abstract reasoning and problem solving. In D.J. Johnson & J.W. Blalock, eds., *Adults With Learning Disabilities.* Orlando, FL: Grune & Stratton.

Swanson, H.L., & B.L. Watson

1982   *Educational and Psychological Assessment of Exceptional Children: Theories, Strategies, and Applications.* Toronto, ON: C.V. Mosby.

Towle, M.

1982   Learning how to be a student when you have a learning disability. *Journal of Learning Disabilities,* 15 (2), 90-93.

Vaughan, J.L.

1984   Concept structuring: The techniques and empirical evidence. In C.D. Holley & D.F. Dansereau, eds., *Spatial Learning Strategies: Techniques, Applications, and Related Issues.* Orlando, FL: Academic Press.

Vogel, S.A.

1987   Issues and concerns in LD college programming. In D.J. Johnson & J.W. Blalock, eds., *Adults With Learning Disabilities.* Orlando, FL: Grune & Stratton.

Wolf, M.

1984   Naming, reading, and the dyslexias: A longitudinal overview. *Annals of Dyslexia,* 34, 87-115.

Index